At Adair's House

At Adair's House

More Columns from America's
Favorite Former Single Mom

ADAIR LARA

FOREWORD BY JON CARROLL
ILLUSTRATIONS BY WARD SCHUMAKER

CHRONICLE BOOKS
SAN FRANCISCO

Printed in the United States of America.

Library of Congress Cataloging-in-Publication Data:
Lara, Adair.
     At Adair's house: more columns from America's favorite
former single mom / Adair Lara.
          p. cm.
     Originally appeared in the San Francisco Chronicle.
     ISBN 0-8118-0498-4 (pbk.)
     I. Title.
AC5.L2 1995
081—dc20   94-33727
                                                  CIP

Cover and interior illustrations: Ward Schumaker
Book design and composition: Gretchen Scoble

Distributed in Canada by Raincoast Books,
8680 Cambie Street, Vancouver, B.C. V6P 6M9

10 9 8 7 6 5 4 3 2 1

Chronicle Books
275 Fifth Street
San Francisco, CA 94103

To Morgan, with love

Contents

FOREWORD
By Jon Carroll

I knew Adair Lara before she was Adair Lara, back when she was just plain old Adair Lara, a magazine editor by profession if not by choice. She and my wife Tracy were sharing an office together, doing similar jobs on different magazines, and they quickly realized they were the only neurotics in a building filled with psychotics. It formed a bond between them; frequently they would go out to lunch and compare notes. "I met this wonderfully funny woman named Adair," Tracy told me one evening. "You'd like her. She may actually be sane."

Adair became a columnist a few years later and, in what seemed like an astonishing coincidence at the time, occupied the space across the page from me in the nether reaches of the *San Francisco Chronicle*. Like everyone else, I was immediately struck by the operatic dimensions of her life. She was a twin, for starters, and being a twin is so inherently crazy-making and otherworldly that it's an almost unworkable premise, for a column or for a life. She had countless brothers and sisters, whole tag teams of nephews and nieces, great advancing hordes of collateral relatives; it was sort of like *Aida*, only without the elephants. And true, all true—that was the astonishing part.

More poignantly, there was her father, the great mystery man in her life and in her work, a living metaphor, by turns shiftless and footloose, always absent but rarely cruel. During the period when he was hiding out in the desert and she was sending him messages in the bottle of the *Chronicle*, hoping he would read how much she wanted him to answer her letters, I felt privileged to watch the tale unfold. It had resonances in my own life; I suspect it had resonances in lots of lives.

Personal journalism is inherently risky. There is no answer to the question: Why should I be interested in this? If you're not, you're not—please move aside. Personal newspaper essays are a peculiarly modern phenomenon, a product of disconnection and alienation. Cynics have said that their popularity (and there are versions to be found everywhere of what Adair does — reality-based television is but a more literal-minded and clumsy version of reality-based column writing) springs from prurience, but I don't believe that. I think their popularity is based on comfort, on connection, on hope. We tell ourselves stories in order to live, as Joan Didion said, and we learn the form of the stories from the myths that surround us.

Too often the myths are impossible to achieve, unuseful, idealized. Our lives do not fit into their comfortable patterns, and we are discouraged. Adair uses her life to say, "look, this is me, this is happening, it's not perfect, I'm confused, I'm dealing with it and wait—here's something we can learn from this muddle. Here's a way of thinking about chaos. Even better, here's a way of *appreciating* chaos."

Adair Lara (and her partially fictional column-writing persona "Adair Lara," who shares everything with the real person except her deepest secrets) is always game for one more go-around. She is often discouraged but never defeated. She is not always wise but she is always clear; she knows what she does not know. She is a character almost as old as American fiction. Adair Lara *is* Huck Finn—the more I think about that, the truer it becomes. She even has freckles on her nose.

Also, there is the matter of class, rarely talked about but always present in American media. Newspapers always seem to speak in the educated, measured tones of the upper middle class. Adair Lara is one of the few authentic working class voices in American journalism; that's one of the reasons she seems to be speaking from a shared past. She is closer to where she came from than many of us are; she knows the way home. I think that's one of the things that makes her column so precious and so useful—she might be a big city girl now, but she grew up poor, collected vices like souvenir ashtrays, started making her mistakes early, fetched up finally with a third marriage and two adolescent children and a deep uneasiness about the sense of serenity she occasionally feels now. She is not smug; she knows it can all go away tomorrow.

A columnist who is not smug; amazing. Try to think of another one.

The effort to recreate herself on paper is intensely conscious. Adair Lara is not a prodigy or a stream-of-consciousness narcissist; she works at her effects and at her prose. Her writing is very careful and very sly; she is in control even when she seems to be just writing a letter home. The work is hard for her, even as the revelations are hard for her; she is in some ways like a great blues singer, tapping into emotions she'd rather forget for the sake of her art. Think of the casual grace of Billie Holiday; Adair's work at its best has the same kind of disciplined longing.

It's all available just beyond this introduction. Best to stop reading this now, best to go forward. Enjoy.

SNARLING
ON THE
BRINK
OF
ADOLESCENCE

Wading Through the Thick of Things

"So, Morgan," I say, plopping down on her bed, "how about if we reorganize your doodad shelves?"

"Hold on a minute, Lily," Morgan says, then turns to me, covering the mouthpiece with her hand. "Mom, get a life." ·

I have a life, thank you. My life is reorganizing closets, listening to maudlin rock songs and looking for the escaped baby mice.

The closets are going very well, and the mice hunting is a moderate success. Our two pet mice went on the lam a couple of weeks ago, but we have their whereabouts narrowed down: They are definitely in the house.

The other night I sneaked into the living room to see the brown mouse racing in an exercise wheel Morgan had left in the middle of the floor. It was 4 a.m., a peak hour here at Mice Nautilus. When it saw me, it cut short its routine and darted under the couch, but now we have a plan, involving the exercise wheel left temptingly inside a trash bag.

The listening to maudlin rock songs, however, is not going well. I haven't even been able to give staring into the middle distance the time it deserves during this bumpy romantic period. If I'd had pets instead of kids, this wouldn't happen. A dog is happy if you just let it look at you, and cats pretend they're just passing through anyway, even if they've lived with you fifteen years. You can stew all day for all they care.

Not so with kids. One of the many disadvantages of having them, next to listening to bad puns and having to do long division all over again, is there's a limit to how unhappy you can be with the likes of them underfoot.

Completely insensitive to your need to stay home and poke holes in the couch, they, in a typical day, haul you out to see *Back to the Future III*, then make you take them back to the mall to buy the "Humpty Dance" tape.

On the way back from the mall, you have to buy a kitten. When you get back in the car, you have to play the "Humpty Dance" tape, trying to make out the dirty lyrics even though the kitten is pleading at the top of its lungs for you to stop the car and let it walk from here.

When you get home, you can't brood in the bedroom because the girl child has flung herself at your phone to complain bitterly to a friend that you stole her "Humpty Dance" tape.

The living room is out because the other child has got himself a sharp knife and is busily building the new kitten, Mike, a house out of the cardboard box the new TV came in, and because Mike himself is padding around, torn between having a nervous breakdown and finding out what's rustling behind the stove.

The kitchen might have worked, despite that rustling, if Patrick had been able to find the right sort of rock. Instead he put a toy convertible Volkswagen in the aquarium, and one of the newts has taken to sitting in the front seat, his front leg hanging casually out the driver's door.

You can't have a decent sinking spell in the same room with a joyriding newt.

Nor can you, it seems, even in bed. When you have at last chased the kids to bed and shown a skeptical Mike his nice RCA box, and are looking forward to lying awake while the clock ticks away the hours, there, curled around your favorite pink pillow and fast asleep, is a child.

It's the same child who had just been declaring, in its own room, that it couldn't sleep a wink if you paid it (which you were willing to do). Now all you can do is snuggle in and steal back a little of the pillow, and fall asleep yourself, knowing that whatever else is true, you certainly do have a life.

You Better Be Good, You Better Not Lie

Back when I was expecting my first baby, people said, "The children will change your life." I thought, sure, people are going to feel free to bombard me with clichés from now on.

But my life did change, because I got it into my head, in my earnest modern-mom way, that you must never lie to children. I forgot that every rule has an exception.

I forgot about Santa Claus.

I don't even know where I got this idea. I had always had a casual code of ethics. What passed for a kind of servile goodness in me as a child was simply a desperate ploy to make myself stand out in a crowd of siblings.

When I grew up I was law-abiding, but perhaps likely to let things slide, to get along, to change the rules when I got tired of them. A project was something you began with high hopes and then abandoned. The traffic laws were suggestions. Nothing had permanence.

Then Morgan came along, followed in a year and a half by Patrick, and something had changed. I got it into my head that one thing in my life would be absolute, unswerving, for sure: Although I might go on telling social fibs to other people, I would never lie to the kids.

I liked the idea of being able to say to them when they were grown: "You know, I never lied to you. Not once, not about anything."

I won't say it was easy. When Morgan was fourteen months old I absent-mindedly handed her a piece of candy, something her dad and I had promised each other she would never taste. "Whaazzat?" she asked. I knew if I gave her the word she would tell her dad. I didn't lie, though I muttered it as indistinctly as I could: "Candy."

"Candy!" she said, all the way home. I had to wrap her face in her muffler when her dad came to lift the stroller up the steps. "Canddyhuh!" she said through it.

It got harder. Years later I told them the divorce was Mommy's idea, though I would have been happier to pin it on Daddy. Telling the truth to them became a habit.

Then one year when he was very small, Patrick went through the house on Christmas morning, hunting for packages from Santa. His dad had warned him that Santa knew he lived in two houses and might decide to drop off the presents at his dad's, but Patrick looked anyway. He found only packages from mom and her friends.

"Don't you believe in Santa Claus, Mom?" he asked as I was sweeping the kitchen floor.

The habit of not lying was too strong. I leaned on my broom. Feeling more as if I were robbing Patrick than as if I were telling him the truth, I said, "No, Patrick, I don't. Santa's just a story."

He looked skeptical. "Just a story?" he said.

"Yes, just a story. There's no such thing as Santa Claus."

Patrick considered this. "Maybe he got lost," he said.

He didn't believe for a minute that Santa Claus didn't exist. He still lived in a magical world, one where a man in a furry suit can be everywhere at once on Christmas Eve, and he wasn't ready to leave it.

Bill remembers how it felt to live in that world. When he was seven and heard that the actor who played Superman on TV had killed himself, he spent days trying to figure out how the actor had done that. Guns wouldn't work, obviously. Had Superman eaten Kryptonite?

If I had to answer Patrick's question again, what would I do? I honestly don't know. I still don't think it's a good idea to lie to kids, but I cringe when I remember it: the day I led my child to believe there was no Santa Claus, when everybody knows there is.

Kids Want No Part of Gender Neutrality

When the babies were born—first a girl, then a boy—my husband, Jim, and I, well-evolved San Francisco parents, were confident that we could bestow on our children enlightened views of their sexual roles.

We began by being very careful to set the proper examples. Far from collapsing in front of the game with a beer, Jim did all the shopping, cooking and sewing. "Anybody who can read can sew," he declared, and made the baby a pair of red crawlers, then moved on to making pillows. All our friends got pillows for Christmas.

It seemed to work. When Patrick was three and another boy ripped his pants, Patrick said sympathetically, "You should get your daddy to fix that for you."

I couldn't tinker with the carburetor or put a new deck on the house, being unfortunately as inept in those areas as in the kitchen, but I could catch and throw and ride a bike pretty well. I was the one who taught Patrick to choke up on the bat and step into his swing, while Jim taught Morgan how to sew and make tuna casseroles.

We were so liberal that we were prepared in advance to accept any aberration. The kids could come to us and confess to be attracted to three-toed tree sloths, and we'd not only understand—we'd more than understand. We'd read all the right literature, find them a support group, join the Parents of

Kids Who Want to Marry Three-Toed Tree Sloths. We'd serve cookies to the young sloths who came calling, and revel in our broad-mindedness.

All of this, this gentle eddying stream of parental enlightenment, was a waste, a roar of sound on the tiny, deaf ears of the little stereotypes we were raising.

I have on a sheet of paper an early but typical dinner conversation across our enlightened table. Morgan, four, remarked over her papaya, "Patrick looked like a girl all day today. That's a girl's sweater."

Patrick, three, was incensed. "I looked like a *boy*," he said. "I have a boy's round face and a boy's round hand."

We gave Patrick a doll. He used it as a launching pad for his Hot Wheels.

Morgan took one look at the other girls in preschool and came home to ask, with an accusing stare, where *her* dresses were.

I would have taught her to step into her swing, too, but she wasn't interested. Now she's twelve, and wears tons of makeup on her already perfect face. She goes to parties and aces the latest dances but shoots the basketball like a girl, or as she imagines a girl does it, which is badly. Her friend Marjanne takes her out for Saturday morning manicures and expensive haircuts.

Patrick, eleven, speaks in a low voice and is always looking for something he can light on fire. "Do you need this Crisco, Mom?" He and his friend Gino sit in the backseat asking each other if they'd rather die from being stabbed or being shot or from being eaten by a shark.

These days Morgan has taken to giving me advice on makeup, even dabbing peach eye shadow on my lids as the car wheels around curves en route to a party. She is sure I can be taught how to be more of a girl if I would just concentrate, and not fidget so much, and let her take me shopping.

Patrick, meanwhile, grabs his dad's apron away from him and drags him to the ball field, showing him how to use two hands to keep the ball from falling out of his mitt.

They figure it's an uphill battle, getting us to embrace our proper roles, but they'll keep at it.

The Only Good TV Is a Dead TV

A month ago, I turned off the cable to the TV, over Morgan and Patrick's vehement protests.

At first we missed it only a little. Morgan discovered the TV sort of works without the cable, on one or two channels, and I'd catch her doing her homework in front of a grainy jumping segment of news. Patrick played Nintendo until he was sick of it, and I found myself pawing through a pile of old tapes one afternoon, looking for something to watch the way a smoker digs through an ashtray, looking for butts.

Then the kids started getting mad. "Why'd you have to do that, Mom?" Patrick grouched.

They would get up on Saturday morning, their hair sticking up, and sleepwalk to the couch, turning their faces to the TV out of old habit.

But the TV was now mute, like a hostage with a rag in its mouth. It was a friendly hearth fire suddenly doused.

What I had imagined was this: The kids, forcibly deprived of their crutch, would grumble for a while, then discover other ways to pass their finite childhood hours.

I forgot that their dad next door and our neighbor Marjanne and all their friends would still have TVs. Their houses would still be filled with color, movement and canned laughter, while in mine the silence would be broken only by the sound of someone turning the pages of a book.

"I hate to say this, but you're making us want to be at Daddy's," Morgan, twelve, said.

"I just got the new TV and VCR," their dad said, doubtfully, when I hinted that my plan wouldn't work unless he axed his set too. "How would I be able to watch 'Masterpiece Theatre'? "

Discouraged, I started to talk to the kids about bringing the box back on a limited basis. "We'll take a vote and not watch sit-coms if there's a good movie on another channel," Morgan said happily.

"Sure," I said, and sighed. Here we go again. It seemed so important to get the TV out, and I make so few good clean hard decisions.

Then Patrick came home from a week in Minnesota, all TV blasted out of him by tingling snowy air, hunting with his cousin, snow sledding, looking for squirrel tracks. He volunteered to watch no TV until June if it means he can go back to Minnesota in the summer.

Our evenings began to pick up. I had bought a book, *What to Do After You Turn Off the TV*. One night, we tried out some of its games, including a funny message for the phone machine. Patrick was unexpectedly good at his lines.

One night, Patrick started looking for that computer typing game we used to have, and Morgan asked me to teach her to iron. It would have been one of those tender moments, if only I knew how.

We played Dictionary, in which you invent false definitions for words no one has ever heard of. Patrick defined "kithara" as "a melting liquid coming from linoleum tiles" and "infusorian" as "the polyester used to make snowsuits." These talents of his hadn't emerged while we were all slumped on the couch watching "Doogie Howser" together.

I find that I'm reading novels at 7 p.m., instead of only in the sleepy minutes before conking out. Getting rid of the TV is like being handed back a chunk of lifetime that someone had taken away. "Here are your evenings back. Enjoy."

The cable people sent me a bill for $278 for their equipment.

I told them to come get the damned thing.

The Homework Cartel

"Where is your homework?" I asked Patrick as he sat on the couch last night with his hands hanging down. "Somebody stole it," he said. "It was right in my pocket."

I shivered. We live in the Duboce Triangle in San Francisco. With several schools nearby, it's a favorite turf for the dread spelling-homework gangs.

It's not the first time we've been hit. Yesterday, Morgan was relieved of her lunch money by a cartel that cruelly planted candy wrappers in her pocket to cover their tracks. They also got the sweatshirt of mine she borrowed ("I put it down for one minute and somebody stole it, Mom!"). Just this morning, they came in right under our noses and made their escape undetected. "Somebody stole my purple brush," Morgan wailed when I told her to brush her hair so we could get going. "I just had it, and now someone stole it."

These are desperate times we live in. My favorite sweatshirt is probably on an unmarked truck speeding toward the border on the interstate. Somewhere else, a forger is crouched over Patrick's spelling list, substituting alternate spellings that will make it untraceable.

Even now, a criminal with lines of bitterness etched around his mouth is standing in a smoky back room, nervously looking all around before handing over the goods from beneath his jacket.

"Watcha got for me, Eddie?" "Girl's hairbrush." "Nah, I can't move these any more. Can't go better than five on this. What else?"

"Just these spelling words."

"Fer Chrissake, that's more like it. I can use all of these you can get me."

The police are helpless in matters like these. It's up to each family to take matters into its own hands. If I want these kids to—dream on, mom—accept responsibility for losing things, or at least to come up with more creative excuses, I just have to . . .

I don't believe it. I had the perfect idea for solving the whole problem, and somebody just stole it!

Confessions of the Publicly Educated

Bill was appalled when I first told him I sent the kids to public school. He couldn't for the life of him see why I would do that when I could, with some scraping, send them to a decent private institution.

I have seen this astonishment on the faces of friends before. Everybody knows you can't get a good education at a San Francisco public school. Taxpayers have been forking over 40 percent of the state budget since forever, and Johnny still can't read. Didn't I care about my kids at all?

I do care about them. I don't know about Johnny, but Patrick and Morgan and I can all read, and we learned to do it in public school.

When I was little, that was where everybody went, except the very wealthy. I went to Lagunitas School out in West Marin, a tiny grammar school lying in a field of poppies. The music program was a cardboard box of battered instruments, and my special tracking consisted of dragging my desk into the hall to go ahead in the arithmetic book.

But I learned to read and write, studied the Constitution, built relief maps of the United States out of clay and memorized "Whose Woods These Are I Think I Know."

This was before busing, loss of local control over schools and the tax revolt. "Your kids won't get what you were getting in school, because we have heard a great deal from taxpayers who don't want to pay for things they consider frills," said one disheartened superintendent.

He might be right. Morgan's in the eighth grade at Everett Middle School, and Patrick's in the sixth. The principal, Linette Porteous, helps out in the cafeteria at lunchtime. The art teacher spends a lot of his time scrounging for markers, three-hole punches and pencil sharpeners. One parent bought duct tape to repair instrument cases and got an impassioned letter of gratitude in return.

The day I talked to her, Linette Porteous was all excited. She and some parents had a truck and were going over to see what good junk Chevron had set aside for schools in an Emeryville warehouse. "What they throw out is better than anything we've seen in years," she said.

In between scrounging missions, Everett's teachers go on teaching. Patrick came home from Judy Logan's composition class and cautioned me to use concrete detail when I write. Morgan was convinced she was no good at math until she landed in Miss Nogara's class.

All the time while the taxpayers have turned away in sorrow, withholding the carpenter's glue and the counselors and sports programs, the schools have gone right on doing the job, teaching these young people who will be running the city when the rest of us are geezers.

I went to a meeting about high schools. Like practically everybody there, I had come with the sole purpose of shoehorning my kid into Lowell, one of the top ten high schools, public *or* private, in the country, but I was astounded at the quality of our other public school options.

We could get a very reluctant Morgan into Burton, which prepares you to enter any college in the country. She can go to the High School of the Arts (over my dead body), or to any number of others.

I can't imagine how these schools got to be good, unless somebody has, all along, gone on giving a damn about the public schools.

My Kingdom for a Jellybean

It's morning, and Morgan and Patrick are trying, in their quiet, civil way, to divide a sack of jellybeans.

"I hate every inch of your body. I'd like to tear your little neck off," Morgan tells her brother. "But I'm a reasonable person, so I'm going to explain my plan to you one more time, so you can understand it perfectly."

"You're so stupid, Morgan," Patrick says mildly. He's lying on his bed, waving his legs idly in the air.

"I say we separate them into piles of each kind of jellybean," Morgan continued as if he hadn't spoken, "then divide the piles equally in half, with all the leftovers going in another pile. Then we divide the leftover pile, and give the extra jellybean to Mom, if there is one."

I'm at my desk, half listening to this, which has been going on for a while. I hid the jellybeans and told the kids they couldn't have them back until they figured out a way of peacefully dividing them. If they couldn't agree, I announced, they couldn't have the jellybeans at all.

Half of me wants the kids to find a way to agree on a way of dividing the jellybeans, and thus learn from the experience, and half of me wants the negotiations to break down completely, so I won't have to produce the bag.

I got up early and ate rather a lot of the jellybeans while reading the paper.

So I'm not being particularly helpful. "Do what the king did when he had one kingdom to divide between two sons," I suggest. "One of you divides the jellybeans, and the other takes his pick."

"Yeah, Morgan," Patrick says, kicking her.

My plan is to let the yelling go on a little longer, then get mad and confiscate the jellybeans.

"Why do you have to divide them exactly that way?" Patrick asks Morgan. "Why not do what I want to do, and take turns choosing until they're all gone?"

"Because this is the way Rachel and Cleo divided their jellybeans," Morgan said fiercely. "I want to divide them the way they did."

So I was not the only one in the room with a secret agenda. Wars are lost, nations betrayed, vital talks sabotaged because a key player has a deeply held, secret idea about the way jellybeans should be divided—or a hidden reason for wanting to sabotage the whole process.

"Why didn't you tell us that in the beginning?" I ask Morgan.

She bursts into tears. "Why should I say so? Why can't you just do it my way? I'm a generous person. I let people have sips of my drinks," she rages, irrelevantly.

"You're crying, so I'll give in to your stupid plan," Patrick says in disgust.

Reluctantly, I go get the paper sack of jellybeans from the top of the bookshelf.

"There were more! Where are the rest?" Morgan cries.

I say, "Oh, were there?" and wander vaguely off to look for them, as if they might have strayed from the sack.

"Mom, there were five blacks, eight white ones and three of these splotched ones. You ate a whole lot!" Morgan says when I come back.

"I may have had one or two," I allow.

Their heads are bent over the coffee table in total harmony now.

"Mom ate all the burgundy."

"She ate all the blues. The blues are the best."

It's Elbow in the Neck Time Again

The minute we got to the campground and found our cabin, a bare wood shack with a lightbulb and cots, Morgan raced into her bathing suit, applied fresh waterproof mascara, yelled to her friends and ran out.

"Wait," I said, grabbing her by the arm, scrounging in my bag for my own suit. "Give me a minute and I'll come too." We were at Mather, San Francisco's family campground up by Yosemite, and I had been looking forward all summer to time with the kids.

"Sorry, Mom," she said, her eyes sliding past me in that new way. "I promised Rachel and Alex . . ."

And she was gone.

"Meet us for lunch!" I yelled after her, but I don't think she heard.

Over the next couple of days, Patrick came by occasionally, stopping his bike in a cloud of wood chips to report what was for lunch in the dining hall, but I never saw Morgan. She was a shout from the diving raft, a pile of sodden clothing under the bunk bed, dusty crushed Welch cans in front of the cabin.

I missed her, but these days I miss Morgan even when she's around.

Nearly thirteen now, she is sometimes at pains to assure me that she wishes she had time to do what she really wants to do, which is spend time with her mom. But Alex needs her to go to the doctor with her, and she promised Amira they'd make pillows, and she and Sky want to finish the movie they're watching. The prospect of a night with the family means frenzied phone calls, trying to get someone, anyone, to come and stay over.

It reminds me of when she was nine months old and so eager to see everything—to find out what that bright splotch was on the other side of the room—that I could hardly hold her. Other moms got burrowing, arms holding tight. I got an elbow in the neck as she leaned out to see the world, leaning so far forward it was a wonder I never dropped her.

Now it's the elbow in the neck all over again. Everybody says that's the age, better get used to it. And I know it is the age—I watch "Roseanne," I *know* how teenage girls talk to their moms. What I don't know is how to behave back.

Bill and I had a wedding to go to, and Morgan was invited, too. Afraid of giving away how much I wanted her to come, I said, coolly, "Just let us know in plenty of time if you decide to come with us." I said it a lot, but it was all I said.

I wasn't surprised when she decided not to. "OK," I said, and we dropped her off at her dad's. As she climbed out, followed by her girlfriends, she said, reproachfully, "You know, Mom, you never said to me, 'I really want you to come.' " I turned around, astonished, but she was already distant again, grabbing her backpack, moving on.

That helped, somehow. I remembered that despite the elbow in the neck, the frantic wriggling to see whatever was coming next, that baby had never stopped wanting to be picked up, and when she ran from me she always looked back to make sure I was following.

The last night at camp, she came in late and climbed into my bunk. Quickly, almost furtively, she hugged me, and whispered, "Good night, Mom." "Good night," I whispered back.

In the morning she asked me, in that new withering tone, if I was seriously planning to wear that bathing suit down to the lake. I said never mind my bathing suit—what about that mess under her bunk? But I was smiling as I went to breakfast, and I swear she sort of waved at me from across the dining hall.

With almost-adolescents, it's the quality seconds that count.

Taming the Beasts of the Family

I find it calms me to hang up Morgan's clothes, at least those eddying right around my feet, when I come to talk to her about her room.

This time I find a hanger on the vanity, among the combs, empty vials of food dye, hair spray, an overturned bottle of Bill's hair gel, a tape called "The Simpsons Sing the Blues," and a plastic bag of clay.

"When are you going to clean this up?" I say.

Morgan bursts into tears. "Why do you always bring that up when you know it upsets me?" she cries, lying amid a pile of gym clothes, books, a pin saying, "I said no to drugs but they didn't listen," a black wig head and an empty glass.

I hang up one last thing, a crumpled white dress, and retreat downstairs, confused. If I'm so right, why is my child weeping?

Later I overhear Bill murmuring to Morgan. "Why don't you just clean it up?" he says. Morgan says something I can't hear, and he answers, "I don't know why, but it's important to her. Just do it, OK?"

I freeze. They're talking about me as if it were just a question of time before I was found wandering down the sidewalk in my nightgown, muttering to myself and slapping at invisible bugs.

This is not me. I'm not nuts. I don't nag. I'm the one who smiles, hearing Morgan singing in her room. I understand her. "I try to be fair to all my clothes," she told me when she was eight. She was sure that the garments that weren't chosen to be worn for a long time felt the slight.

I understand, yet the mess gnaws at me. Why? I pay for the space, but the rent won't go down if she cleans her room.

I go into her room to turn off her light, wading through ripped magazines, shoes, nail polish, tin foil, pens, two glasses and a biology textbook I've been billed for.

As I wade, a monster stirs, summoned up from the depths by the sounds of a poster getting flattened and a glass rolling across the floor. It's a mother monster, centuries old. The monster knows from suffering, and hard work, and not getting any respect. Every mother born adds to her, a cell of resentment here, a cell of jealousy and regret and dreams never realized there.

The monster doesn't love the child. She just wants the room cleaned up. Pronto.

But Morgan is just shy of thirteen, and not herself either. She can't help the tears: She's channeling an adolescent monster. This monster bears no love for the mom, either. For years, while Morgan smiled her way through middle childhood, this monster has been filing away information on what will irritate me most. The adolescent monster whines, and complains that her home is boring, and demands to go to Haight Street though it'll be dark in half an hour. The monster quivers with the injustice of it and cries with the sheer frustration of being powerless to get her own apartment.

Knowing about the monsters helps us both.

Sometimes mine is stirring, and I make Morgan clean up her mess. Sometimes her monster is huger than mine, and I promise to avert my eyes from the art project smashed into the rug, if only Morgan will agree to hang up her clothes or put them in drawers.

Even her huge monster thinks this is fair. I just went in there, and Morgan has done exactly what I asked: Some of her clothes are attached to hangers, and the rest are in her drawers. The hangers they are attached to are strewn colorfully across the bed, and the drawers lie here and there around the floor, where every item in them has an equal chance of being chosen.

Death Comes to Dinner

It was dinnertime, and we were talking about this and that when Patrick said that his new philosophy was that we should all live for today. "No, Patrick, you cannot have a dirt bike," I said automatically. We all got to talking, and somebody happened to remark, "After all, you only have one life."

Something about that stopped Patrick in his tracks. "What is death?" he wanted to know.

Bill gave it a try. "You know, there was a time, a time your Mom and I and even Morgan can remember, when there was no Patrick. Death is like that—there will once again be a time when there is no Patrick."

Patrick stared at Bill. You could see that sinking in. No Patrick?

I suppose we can all—or all of us raised without the consolation of religion—remember this moment of knowing that you will stop but the world will go on. I recall sitting on a swing when a neighbor kid squatted down and buried a sowbug in the soft dirt. "It's dead as a doornail," he said. I must have looked adequately shocked, for he added, "You're going to die, too, and be buried in the dirt like a sowbug, with the worms eating your eyes."

Like that moment, years later, when someone first explained sex to me, it was repulsive, shocking, and it instantly made sense. For days after I found out about death, I wondered why anybody bothered to go to school, or read anything, or struggled through long division. Why not just lie in bed and wait for it to come?

Then it receded, that terrifying discovery, to a kind of distant rumor. In a way, I stopped believing it.

I guess that had been Patrick's moment, because a few days later he brought it up again, at bedtime. I was bustling around, turning out lights, but he just sat there. "You made me die," he said, when all I was doing was trying to get him to brush his teeth. "I gave you life," I answered. "Yes," he answered bitterly, "so I can die."

So the three of us talked. Morgan told Patrick that he should be worrying about something important, such as were we going to buy him a car when he was sixteen. Then she started coughing loudly—she had that flu that was going around—and I asked her to stop. She fell off the couch and lay on the floor, still coughing. "Don't let me interrupt your little moment, Mom," she said, wryly.

By now I was babbling. I told Patrick that I had read that as you get older, the cells that make you worry begin to die off, and as you get closer to death you worry about it less and less. I told him he would be a very old man when he died, and would leave children behind him to remember him, and perhaps his own good works. The time when there is again no Patrick would not be exactly like the time when there never had been.

Finally, he stopped worrying about it. The cloud passed. But I thought of it again the other day. Patrick had been caught with his bike after dark, and I had followed him home in my car.

As I drove, I watched his T-shirt billowing up over his back as he ostentatiously slowed down at intersections, turning to grin at me. The sight of that bare back made me wonder what good it was supposed to do, my following him. If another car darted out of a side street and walloped him I could do nothing but watch.

The thing is, we both already know that I can't keep him safe. He knows he can ride through the streets just as easily without me.

Still, it made sense to him, that I shepherd him home through the dark with my car. He must already know that it's the little moments like that, strung like lights on a welcoming porch, that hold back the darkness.

Siblinghood Is Powerful

One of the world's most succinct pieces of advice comes from a book on how to avoid sibling rivalry. "Have only one child," it says.

Last night Patrick, eleven, told Morgan, thirteen, that her outfit—Santa Claus boxer shorts over gray sweat pants—was "fingernails on a blackboard." She stole his red blanket, then accused him of not caring about anything or anybody when he demanded it back. Ten minutes later he bought an ice cream at the store, pretended there were more in the fridge, and grabbed her place on the couch when she got up.

Each of them resents every mouthful of food the other eats, every stitch of clothing he owns, the very air the other breathes. I used to tell them that it was impossible to be absolutely equal all the time, but that when they were twenty-one and each added up everything I had ever given them or done for them, every quarter for the bus, every pair of roller skates, they would find it was equal.

They actually bought that.

I thought I was doing Morgan a favor when I gave her another child to grow up with. I even made it a point to have them close together.

I should have remembered from my own childhood that a sibling is another rank weed to fight with for sun and water.

I had six brothers and sisters, and we had no more regard for one another than puppies in a litter. Everything they got was something I didn't get. Every smile at one child was an arrow in a sibling's heart. After Sean was born, my parents had four girls in a row in an attempt to provide him with a brother, and when Shannon finally came along Sean did his best to enlarge the room they shared by using Shannon's head as a battering ram.

Connie, born second, then presented ten months later with a nice sister to play with, drew a yellow line across the floor of the room she shared with Mickey and dared her to cross it. Just the sight of Mickey's blond curls made Connie pull more stuffing out of the mattress they shared.

I was never what you would call friends with any of them. Connie was cranky, rolling her hair in Minute Maid cans behind a locked door. Sean and Mickey were too old to talk to me, Shannon and Robin were too young for me to talk to them.

Even Adrian, my twin, was a mystery to me, locked away in her own world, as I was locked away in mine. I had no idea what she was like, what she was afraid of, or what she thought of me. I knew that she liked Lorna Doones and could run faster than anyone else in the third grade, and that later Mother was always trying to get her to pose for pictures in her bathing suit, even when I was already posed winningly on my towel, trying to get her attention.

Then we all grew up. Connie and Mickey still don't talk to each other. The yellow line is now the state border between Idaho and Utah. I don't see much of my brothers, though I wish I did. But I have four sisters.

They'll still be here when my parents are gone and my children have families of their own. We will still be on the phone to one another every day, checking in with one another as we move through life.

He doesn't know it now, but Patrick is going to like having a sister. And Morgan is going to like having a brother.

They'll come together to visit me when I'm a wheezing old thing in the rest home, and I'll give them their lists of every single thing they ever got from me.

They'll see that it was equal, for at the top of his list it'll say, "A Sister," and at the top of hers, "A Brother."

The Best of Ages, the Worst of Ages

I can hear my own voice ringing in my ears, smugly telling people that every time the kids get a year older, I think this is it—this is the very best age of all.

It started when I was pregnant. People said, "Better enjoy yourself now, because your life will change when the baby comes." When the baby arrived, and I sat there dopily smiling down at her and taking her blithely off to restaurants, they said, "Well, sure, she's just a baby. But wait until she can walk."

I didn't have to wait long. When she was nine months old I looked up from my desk to see the top of a blond head moving past the desk, like a cantaloupe bobbing in the current. A week later she was running in Golden Gate Park, chasing balloons.

"OK, OK," they said, "but wait 'til she's *two.*"

Morgan at two. We took her tearfully over to preschool and waved good-bye. When we went back to pick her up, instead of rushing over she yelled cheerfully, "Hi, Dad! I'm walking in a line!"

Wait until she gets interested in boys, they said. Wait, wait, wait.

Then they said, wait until she's a teenager.

Morgan turned thirteen in November.

She calls at 6:30 to say she's watching a movie at Rachel's, she lost track of the time. When I yell at her, she looks at me with eyes like rocks. When all I want to do is fix her collapsed bed so she can sleep in it, she tells me, crossly, to go away and leave her alone. I tell her to come home after school, and she says, "You act as if I have to do anything you say." She demands to be allowed to take buses late at night.

I wouldn't feel so low about this, but it's also been a week since she stashed the red shorts in my room. It started when I kept trying to give her some red gym shorts as she was leaving for school. She kept saying they were Patrick's, but I wasn't really paying attention, and I stuffed them in her back-pack anyway.

That night I found them in my shoes. I put them on her lamp. They turned up two days later stretched across a picture above my bed, and I flew them out her two-story window like a flag. Neither of us has ever said a word about the shorts.

Last week was particularly trying. Morgan's report card looked like spilled alphabet soup—and from the wrong end of the alphabet. When her dad went to pick Morgan up at a party, the girls seemed all upset over some-thing, and Morgan said, "We can't leave yet, Daddy. We're crying."

She burst into tears again a day or two later when I said her six girlfriends couldn't spend the night. When they left, I heard her begging them to stay, or to invite her over, anything to get her out of an evening at home with the family. I invite her to see "Wayne's World," but she says she wants to see it *with* someone. In the morning I never see her: She is a distant radio, a clomping overhead, an outstretched hand needing money for the bus, a voice saying, "What happened to that phase you were going through, of making us nice lunches?"

On top of everything else she's been asking all week why I never wear my Chronicle sweatshirt anymore. I say, "What do you care, you know you can't borrow it," in that new peevish way I have of talking to her.

Crossly, I pick up the juice boxes and frozen-burrito wrappings that mark Morgan's passage through the house, then jerk my Chronicle sweatshirt off the hanger, and put it over my head.

My arm won't go through the sleeve.

There, rolled up in the arm, are the red shorts.

I knew I was going to like this age most.

When Illness Was a Thing to Celebrate

It was Bring Out Your Dead week at my house last week. Bill and I, weakened by stressful house hunting and by a treasure hunt in a rainstorm, were felled by vicious colds.

It was pitiful. We holed up in his Russian Hill digs for three days, using kitchen knives to get cold capsules out of their terrorist-proof packages and arguing about whether it's better to suffer without cold remedies or whether to, in my view, take everything that isn't nailed down, on the off chance it might do some good.

"You're about twelve hours behind me," Bill said. "Your hair looks better than mine."

We were sick, and nobody could do anything about it. When you're grown up, getting sick means nothing more than feeling rotten and getting behind on your work.

It's different with kids. When the squeeze and I started getting better, the blizzard of Kleenex tapering off into occasional flurries, Morgan, twelve, came down with a killer combo of strep throat and chicken pox. "Stop grinning like that," her dad told her when she heard she was quarantined from school. "It isn't good news."

But it was. I knew exactly how she felt. As a kid, I loved getting sick. I got to stay on the green couch in the kitchen and eat Neapolitan ice cream while the warm kitchen world buzzed around me. A saucepan was tucked under the couch for my throwing-up pleasure, and Mother came over some-times to lay a cool hand on my forehead.

The ordinary order was upset: There was ice cream for lunch, bed blankets were dragged to the couch and I got to enter that mysterious world, the house when I wasn't in it. When the other kids came home, jealous as puppies, they were told to lower their voices because I was sleeping.

I felt myself lifted up, made to feel different, special.

Morgan, very ill by the second day, covered with itchy spots, asked me to read to her. Busy, still sick myself, I said, "I will, but I want you to do some-thing about your room first."

"I'm supposed to have a sponge bath," she answered miserably, and wandered off.

Next minute, I heard her on the phone. She had called her dad next door. "Oh, nothing," I heard her say. "Just wanted to see what you were doing."

I knew why she called him. He's one of those people who know how much an ailing human wants to hear someone say, "What are you doing *up?* Get back to bed immediately, while I make you some hot tea!" He used to tuck me into bed with a lovely unabridged *War and Peace* while he brought me his own mother's cure, a steaming bowl of hot milk with butter floating in it.

Sitting there, listening to Morgan talk to her dad, I remembered that I still feel it now and then, bizarrely, that little undercurrent of joy that rises at the onset of a sniffle—"Yippee! I'm sick!" It's as if any minute a magic carpet will arrive to take you back to that green couch, that bite of cardboardy Neapolitan, that feeling of being warm and safe and looked-after.

It's as if, once a child has been properly coddled, the magic carpet is built in.

"Morgan? How about a sponge bath?"

We brought every pillow in the house into the living room. I brought Morgan lemon yogurt in a chilled champagne glass, and squished warm water over her on a green towel, with the heat blasting.

We lay on the pillows and watched terrible movies all day, until even I was kind of getting into it, how nice it can be to be sick.

It's Not Time to Let Go

I don't know where Morgan slept last night. She yelled at her dad on the phone when he told her to come home and went off with friends instead. I have a pretty good idea where she is, but I don't absolutely know for sure, because they take the phone off the hook over there.

I can imagine what you must be thinking. What kind of mother is she? So would I, last year. Now I'm the mother of a teenager, and all I can say is, I had no idea it would be like this.

This all started suddenly this spring, the sneaking out to be with friends and the outrageous lies to cover up.

I know this is typical, that adolescents have to reject the parents they love to break away. My own friends tell funny stories of what they did at the same age. Kathy's dad quit going to bed at all, but just took catnaps in a chair for three years after he discovered that Kathy was calling cabs in the middle of the night to meet her boyfriend.

On the other hand, this is the city, and I'm scared. Morgan went on the lam one night a couple of months ago and was grounded for two weeks—no friends, no phone, no TV, nothing.

It was worth it, she says. It was hella-fun. Even the part where they went into Dolores Park at 2 a.m., where the drug dealers hang out. And the part where someone in the Safeway parking lot gave them beer.

"You don't have to worry about the park, Mom. Oh, I know they hang out there. But this was perfectly safe. The cops had just been there and everything. They wouldn't hurt us. And if they tried, we'd kick them in the you-know-where. My friends wouldn't let anything happen to me.

"Stop rolling your eyes, Mom. God, you used to be such a cool mom. OK, so I'm grounded, you don't have to act all mad."

I spent last evening wandering around the house, in between calls. My errands keep taking me into Morgan's room, where I recognized several pairs of her dad's jeans in the carpet of clothing covering the floor. The kids are all wearing their clothes several times too big now, so they borrow them from us. They walk around swaddled in our clothes.

Like a jilted lover, whose own feelings have not changed, I read Morgan's verses, scribbled on binder paper and scattered across the bed. The bad spelling cheers me up.

On the floor I find a note from a friend of Morgan's whose parents have stopped speaking to her. "All they're going to do is clothe me and feed me," says the sad note. The mother of another boy I know is sending him to relatives in the Midwest because she can't handle him. He's a wonderful boy, handsome, good at talking to adults. Last year I would have thought, jeez, can't you handle your own child? Don't you care about him?

I have changed a lot. Now I think how it must feel, not to speak to your own child, or to send him away. I think how much must have happened, for it to have come to that. Now when a friend of Morgan's says her mom doesn't care where she is, I have my doubts.

I am not so quick to judge, now.

"Just let her go," a friend urges. "See how she likes that."

Just let her go. They say that's the story of raising a child: Pick me up, hold me tight, put me down, let me go.

I'm not ready to do that. I'm going to find that kid, and ground her good, and then ground her again. We have new locks for the house, and we mean business.

She's only thirteen, and I'm still at hold me tight.

Gifts for Mom: The Teen Years

I was sitting at the pool at my mother's complex, feeling pretty good. For Mother's Day, I gave Mom a very nice voice-activated tape recorder, a box of popular songs on cassette, a bag of croissants, and two slightly battered eight-track tapes and a green baseball cap.

Then my brother Shannon, that showoff, arrived with a present he had to borrow a truck to bring over: a new Ping-Pong table that he set up in the carport. This from the same kid who gave Mother an electric carving knife about five years after she had last cooked anything. She made him take it right back to the store.

I don't think she'll make him take the Ping-Pong table back.

"So, what'd *you* get?" Mother asked me, brushing a leaf off her new Ping-Pong table.

Well, if you must know, I said, my presents are all still at school, drying. Much too big to be moved. Or so I'm told.

Patrick had stayed over at a friend's, but when I woke up on Mother's Day I still had one child left to fake a little gratitude for thirteen years of care and comfort. I had heard Morgan indignantly scolding her friend Steve on the phone that morning, "But it's *Mother's Day!* Aren't you going to spend it with your mother?" (This from a girl who the night before had said to the same boy, "No, I'm home all by myself tonight. Well, Bill and my mom are home.")

So I guess I was the tiniest bit let down when there was nothing actually on the table when I came down in the morning, ready to go wild over my cards and school-made flower vases. Not that I remotely cared about getting presents, of course. Honestly, it's enough, the satisfaction of having raised a pair of lazy, good-for-nothing, ungrateful . . . I stomped upstairs to find Morgan luxuriating on her bed in a pool of sunlight. "Clean up this mess," I said, by way of good morning. "But it's Mother's Day," she protested, not moving.

"Oh, is it?" I said. I went downstairs to sulk on the back porch. I stared out the window at the cherry tree, my heart as shrunken and hard and disappointed as the fruit on that neglected tree.

"Where are you, Mom?" she called.

"Here," I said. My voice was thin and bitter. I had no idea I liked those paper vases, those cards with ribbons glued in them, the table decorated with weeds before I came down to breakfast. Two years ago I was wakened at six when the kids brought in a cake and made me eat a slice on the spot, before I even got up.

Morgan came up. She was wearing my white tank top. I would have to pitchfork through the piles on her floor to get it back. "Did you do your room?" I said.

She ignored that. She sat down, unruffled. "Look," she said. She showed me a plaster relic in a shoe box. It was of the red shorts we have been hiding in each other's stuff all during this difficult spring, a spring of surly answers, sneaking out of the house and sideways looks.

And that was just me. She was worse.

"See where it broke?" she said. "I've been trying to glue them back all week." She had, too. Bill found his tube of glue, open, down by the door to the laundry room. "And I have a painting of the shorts at school, all different sizes, all colors of red. I couldn't bring it home because we had class soutside and I couldn't get back in."

"That would have been good," I said, still sulkily. But I liked it, the idea of a ceramic of the red shorts, and the painting. It's almost as good as cake at dawn.

When we got in the car to go to my mother's, there were the red shorts, stretched out on the steering wheel.

Starting High School for the Second Time

Rap music blasted in my ears as I drove Morgan through the swirling fog over Portola Drive to school. I couldn't stop talking. "Do you have your lunch money? Where's your jacket?" I said, turning down the music so I could be heard.

It was her first day of high school. I had to talk, had to babble about my own first day at Drake High in San Anselmo, with my stupid new Sassoon haircut, a cut on my lip that bled whenever I started talking to someone, and six classrooms to find. I was a freshman, the lowest worm of all the worms. But I had a locker, and I got to dress down, and elementary school seemed infinitely in the past.

I had been there, and I knew the last person you want to see or be seen with at this time is your mother, hanging around like a reminder of baby-hood.

"Can we talk later?" Morgan said, reaching over to turn the radio back up.

I reached over to turn it back down. I had brought her this far, and I was entitled to my moment, darn it.

With your firstborn, you never really get a handle on this new emotion, on the way you feel about your children. It's a storm that never passes. Every event in their lives is an event in yours. You measure the very length of your own motherhood by their age.

Crowds of kids were streaming along Eucalyptus Drive as we approached Lowell High. It doesn't look like much—a dismal collection of buildings shrouded in fog—but it's been around since 1856. Morgan says when she tells her friends she's going to Lowell, they say, "What are you supposed to be, smart or something?"

Morgan's getting antsy now, wants me to slow to about 30 miles an hour and let her leap before anybody realizes she has a mom. I want to take her by the hand, lead her in, squeeze into her seat with her.

But she's on her own here, one of 3,000 kids. Thanks to budget cuts, Lowell students are urged to get used to writing notes if they want to talk to a counselor, of whom there are three. Her dad and I went to parents' night: They inform you that your freshman will be doing homework from now to kingdom come and will be lucky to get D's. And they were talking to parents of hard-working students, students who already have their own sets of encyclopedias.

I was sufficiently alarmed to buy Morgan a desk for her room. It arrived on a Friday, unassembled, packed in a box weighing 176 pounds. Morgan kept wanting to put pieces of it together, and I kept worrying that she'd wreck it. I told her to wait until her dad had time to help.

But every time I went into her room more of the desk was done—first the file drawers, then the cabinets. I'd say as I was leaving, "Don't do any more now," but she'd already be reading more of the directions.

On Sunday morning I walked into her sunny room and saw the desk, finished, with a jar of flowers and two radios on it. Morgan was asleep on the bed, fully dressed.

I remembered this now, as I turned the car around and sped away, with Morgan getting smaller in the rearview mirror. This was Morgan's moment, not mine. It was never mine.

Waltzing Through Life with a Teenager

Boy, she scared me. Morgan, I mean. Starting when she was twelve, with her gaze traveling past me in that new way, and then the lying, the outbursts, the dropping notes from her bedroom window to kids on the street below, the waltzing defiantly out the door when I had said she couldn't go.

Suddenly, living with her was like having my own personal brick wall. "*Why* do I have to have a curfew?" she'd say. "It solves nothing! I'll just come home when I'm ready, probably by 7:30 but I can't say for sure."

When I insisted she do homework, she was puzzled. "Why should I have to do homework when you say I do? You don't even know if I *have* homework. You've never gone to my school."

She warned her dad and me not to expect too much of her first report card, as we had been upsetting her a lot lately. "You're so mean now!" she cried. "You never used to be this way." It's true I had started to sound a lot more like other moms than I did like myself. I was unreasonable, but I had little choice: The reasonable response to a lot of what a teenager says is to stare incredulously, make a sarcastic remark, then lock her in her room until she's thirty, sliding cold pancakes under the door.

I had always handled her easily, made her laugh, and for the first time I was unsure of my footing. We hauled her off to counselors. I had the name of a no-nonsense boarding school in Nevada City, and my sister standing by in Idaho, with a spare bedroom. Scared, uncertain, I retreated once more to books, as I had the time she was four weeks old and started to cry for hours at night with colic. When I read, then, that it was mostly the nervousness of first-time moms that made colicky babies, I put the "Beer Barrel Polka" on the stereo and waltzed her gently around the living room, holding her tight but still deliberately relaxing my arms.

"This is you, not me," I crooned to her. "I'm not upset about this at all, myself. We're just dancing." Her colic disappeared.

My deepest fear came from stories from women who said they battled with their mothers so much as teenagers that they never felt close to them again. One of them wrote to me: "Everything you have to teach her, you have already taught her. Acknowledge your changed relationship. Discuss her plans for her career and the time and dedication she plans to put into it. Don't freak out if she doesn't have any the first ten times you ask."

It took a while for me, but I got it, I think. I no longer have a girl child to boss around and watch over, but an undisciplined but funny fourteen-year-old—er—adult living in the bedroom behind the kitchen.

Morgan now comes home more or less on time, does her homework, is doing fine at school. We go by my rules—I'm the mom—but otherwise I try to treat her as I would any friend, respecting her judgment in clothes and makeup and boyfriends, struggling to stay silent about her food choices, wanting to hear about her experiences, even the scary ones. "Promise you won't be mad if I tell you . . ." some of her conversations begin, and I brace myself. "I promise I won't be mad."

It's not always easy, having a fourteen-year-old buddy. She's the only friend I have who considers getting the phone her share of housework, does everything she can to get out of my company, makes terrible jokes, borrows my Gap jeans without asking and then lends them to friends, and never ever picks up the check.

"That's all right," I say to her, silently, as she gabs away on the phone. "This is not about me, this is about you. We're just dancing."

The Search for the Coolest Sweatshirt

When I went in to wake Morgan for school for the third time, she was lying in bed. "What're you doing?" I said.

"Waiting for Daddy to bring me some clothes."

Patrick, meanwhile, was sitting at the kitchen table with his head buried in his arms. "What are *you* doing?" I asked him as I hurried to throw together their lunches.

"I'm thinking about what to wear."

A kid on the brink of teenhood has a new sense of urgency about his clothes. If he wears the same thing more than once in the same week, kids will assume 1) he thinks he looks cool wearing it, or 2) it's one of three outfits he has to his name, and he frantically rinses it out at night.

"What about your black pants?" I said. "I wore them last Thursday," he answered. "Everybody will remember." I asked him what I had worn to the mall when he and I went shopping the night before, and he couldn't remember. I covered his eyes and asked him what I had on right then, and he couldn't remember. But he still won't wear the black pants.

"Maybe I could wear my overalls," he says. "What'd you do with them, anyway?"

When he was younger, Patrick thought you got dressed by raising your arms in the air. He has changed since then, but is still sure I'm behind the appearance and disappearance of his clothes. Now he wants me to perform my old magic, make some cool pants appear.

The overalls are in his drawers, but I've never seen either child resort to looking in his own dresser for something to wear. A sense of defeat seems to settle over them if they have to confine their hunt to such an impoverished local area. I suspect Patrick hasn't opened his dresser in years. The clothes in it fit him when he was six.

Instead, as the clock ticks toward nine, he and his sister fan out, a bleary-eyed, wild-haired duo made vulnerable by the need to look cool. While Morgan heads upstairs to find out what's keeping her dad, Patrick shows up at my desk, carrying my bathrobe so I'll have something to wear after I give him the sweatshirt I've got on.

Everybody can wear everybody's clothes because the fashion calls for kids to dress like bundles of laundry. Patrick got caught at the beginning of the school year with a wardrobe that, uselessly enough, actually fit him, but he can sometimes piece together an outfit from what's on his sister's floor. Today, for example, he found her size 40 white pants, a score worth her usual lecture, delivered at point-blank range, about how generous she is, how he never lends her anything, and how this is the last time he can borrow anything, ever. I stand behind the door, listening, secretly charmed. Aw, listen to that, the kids are sharing.

Sometimes they ask me how they look. I say, "That's great, you look fine, I always liked that shirt on you," and they go off to change again. They know I just want them to get to school on time. Morgan could appear in the kitchen at 8:30 in scuba gear and I'd say, "You look great, nice tank, now go to school."

By the time they leave, the two of them could pose for magazine covers, hair slicked back, sweatshirts hitting them fashionably at midknee. Left alone with the blare of the radio and the lunches forgotten on the table, I am looking a little the worse for wear myself, having been stripped of my sweatshirt and having to search for jeans amid the tiny piles of clothes all over the house. But I'm not a teenager, and I find that clothes matter less and less. In fact I find it's most efficient to wear the same clothes all the time, and just vary the places I go.

As Close to Perfect as a Mom Gets

I am an admirably calm, serene, mature person when I'm alone.

Oh, a fleeting look of impatience may flit across my features when the ringing of the phone breaks my concentration or when I accidentally put my foot in the cat's water dish, but most of the time I am really a kind of Donna Reed, moving through a series of rooms that are as neat as a pin, pausing in a pool of sunlight to tuck a rosebud back into position in a bouquet, calmly wiping up the spilled water from the cat dish.

That's how I see myself when I am alone—as a person whose wonderfulness will last until somebody walks in or phones or in some way tests it.

It is exactly the same way I admire myself as a mother, when there is no teenager present. When the kids are sleeping at somebody else's house, I throw back the covers and prepare for another day as a kind and sympathetic and right-acting mom.

All I have to do is follow my warm human instincts, be my naturally affectionate and encouraging and humorous TV-mom self.

In my imagination, a kid could walk in with a shaved head, or casually let slip that he was tossed out of school or announce that from now on he'd be running his own life, and I'd respond with exactly the right words, encouraging him and setting him straight at the same time.

When the kids aren't around, I could put out a video on being a good mom. I have read books on parenting teens—so many that I've even grown comfortable with the use of "parent" as a verb. I have long funny conversations with my sisters on what Morgan's been up to—"Jeez you'll never believe what she pulled last night."

Anybody looking in the window, seeing me put the phone down from talking to my sister, a smile crossing my face as I shake my head, thinking about those darn kids, would realize I'm not an anxious, crying mom who lives with teenagers—the kind of mom who is always nagging someone and who occasionally, when no one is looking, bursts into tears.

That's not me. I let people wear whatever they like, don't care whether they put the milk away or not, look only mildly pained if they talk giddily of having done something wild and foolish.

You can wear any color lipstick you want around me. As your friend, I might mention that your suspenders have hiked up your pants pretty far in back, but I will only mention it in passing. I don't mind if you eat a burrito at 4:30 when dinner is at 6. Heck, eat whatever you like.

I'm not your mother.

I am, when the kids are absent, like a lot of people who don't have teenagers, but who in their minds know exactly how to deal with them. Who in their minds show them exactly who's boss.

When I'm alone, I'm like myself before I had a teenager and found myself raising my eyebrows at people who let their kids run wild, or threw up their hands at their messy rooms or allowed them to smoke. "Man," I thought when I saw those parents, "get a grip." They're just kids.

When I'm alone, I'm as good at this as those people who don't have teenagers.

It's only when the teenagers come home and are actually in the house, eating bowls of Apple Jacks, watching cartoons, telling me they were late because nobody had a watch and then the bus broke down, that I become a tiny bit less wonderful.

It's only at these times that a lot of what I've learned from books about being calm and encouraging and cool tends to go out the window, and I find myself, instead of hitting exactly the right note of amused tolerance and gentle firmness, standing in front of the TV holding a report card out with tongs or delivering impassioned infomercials on how I felt when I found my new shirt crumpled under an overturned wastebasket.

It's only then I lose my perfect confidence and feel frail, and human, and remember that wonderfulness comes not from being, but from trying.

Parents Had to Work,
Why Not Their Kids?

I've been arguing with the kids a lot lately about their allowance. They want an increase, and I've been thinking of actually decreasing it.

I've been very patient, letting them play on their swing set out in front all these years, but now I want them to find work.

It's a matter of building their character. Baby-sitting on Friday night now will prepare Morgan to take her place at the top of the corporate heap later. Spending Saturdays sweeping wood shavings at a friend's construction site will teach Patrick the satisfaction of money earned. I once read a story about a father who forced his son to cut an enormous expanse of lawn almost blade by blade, with tiny clippers, all one long summer while the boy's friends were playing baseball, and while the father lay dying on the porch. He could think of no better gift for a son he was leaving than teaching him to work.

That was going a bit far, but none of us will be around forever to shell out for the Nikes and the Gap jeans. As we send our kid off to be splattered with ketchup and ordered around by a pimply older kid in a paper hat, we feel good about the lessons that enduring such treatment will teach him.

And we can't help but think of how hard we worked ourselves, as teenagers. Bill washed dishes in an old-age home, mowed lawns for a landscaping company, helped his dad on deliveries, filled shelves as a box boy at the Hilltop Market. He says all getting his driver's license did was expand the ways he could be put to work.

By the time I'd finished high school, I'd sliced tea cake at bingo games, waited tables, whipped up hundreds of Orange Julius shakes, sold Rocky Road candy bars at the pool, cleaned coffee urns at private parties, rotated cakes at Lady Baltimore, spent rainy afternoons at nursery schools helping toddlers into their boots. Adulthood has been a welcome vacation after the long grind of adolescence.

We were no more enthusiastic about working than my own kids are. I remember once telling my mother that I was quitting the Friday night bingo job because I was missing all the parties.

Mother put down her book. "When I was twelve years old, I was packing shoes full time in the basement of the Empire State Building," she said.

I knew this. Every time we kids so much as argued over whose turn it was to take out the garbage, Mom started packing those shoes again. "You kids don't know how easy you have it," she'd say. And I'd keep my job.

Now, as the kids wait for someone to break into the living room and offer them work that won't interfere too much with their social lives, I am forced to remind them that I worked every Friday night putting out coffee and cake at the bingo game.

I don't say it, but it hangs in the air: the assumption that whatever success I've had in life can be traced directly to those sticky tea cakes.

Why should kids work? I can offer only the most unselfish and disinterested of reasons, the most far-reaching of parental guidelines:

Because *we* had to, that's why.

There's nothing unfair about this. They'll have their day. As Morgan stomped off to catch the bus to school yesterday, after failing to persuade anyone to give her a lift, she said over her shoulder, "When I grow up, I'm going to give my kids rides everywhere they want to go!"

But she won't.

Her kid (a teenaged daughter, if there is a God) will ask for a ride. She'll glance up from her book and yawn. "Get real. At your age I got up at 6:30 and took three different buses to school. You don't know how easy you have it."

Am I Turning into My Mother?

In her book, *It's Always Something,* Gilda Radner remembers a dog, about to have puppies, who got in the way of a lawn mower and had to have her hind legs cut off. The vet sewed her up, and she learned to walk by taking two steps and flipping up her backside, then taking two more steps and flipping up her backside again. She had her puppies, nursed them and weaned them.

And when they learned to walk, they walked like her.

Mothers. I tell you.

My daughter, locked me out of the house this morning while I was downstairs doing the laundry. I had it coming—she wanted to stay at a party until 1:00, and I said I'd be there at 11:30.

After a while Bill heard my knocking and thawed me out in the kitchen, where Morgan was eating her Raisin Bran as cool as you please. "Just give me three good reasons why I can't stay out till 1:00," she steamed.

"Because I certainly didn't stay out until 1:00 at your age."

"At my age you were a demented little bookworm with no social life," Morgan pointed out. "Give me another reason."

"Because I said so," I blurted out.

Then I stopped. That didn't sound like me. Who said that?

I remembered a day when I was twelve, and desperate to go to a party. I wailed, I sulked, I followed my mother from room to room, whining, "Give me one good reason why I can't go."

Finally my mother, exasperated, turned and said, "Because I said so, that's why."

This is supposed to make me feel depressed as hell, that I am repeating things my mother said. If a boy turns out like his dad, he's a chip off the old block, but if a girl is like her mother—watch out. The women's magazines are filled with chilling accounts of women who find themselves echoing the person who blighted their own childhoods.

"I discovered my own mother's words coming out of my mouth," a horrified woman told an interviewer in *Glamour* magazine. "I swore I'd never talk to my kids that way."

I swore I'd never do anything my mother did, including the way she would obsessively clean and cook as often as twice a week. When we whined, she'd snap, "Stop that, or I'll give you something to cry about." I used to hear that and think, "I already have something to cry about. What could she mean? A prize?" So I'd cry harder, hoping to win the prize.

She'd tell us again about how when she was thirteen she went to work packing shoes in the basement of the Empire State Building. "You kids don't know what work is," she'd say, oblivious to the fact that she was blocking our view of the television set.

But that isn't all I remember. Mother would also say, "Are you warm enough in that sweater?" or "Oh, geez, don't worry about it. I did the same thing at your age." She was always saying, "It's a beautiful day out. Maybe we finish this later, and go to the beach?"

She said a lot of smart, calming things that I would be pleased to discover coming out of my own mouth. A lot of things I would like Morgan to hear.

I'm going to give Morgan some tips on turning into me. It would be just like her to forget important details, like how reasonable I was about her curfew, on the days when I wasn't locked out of the house.

Does
Bill
Know?

Looking for Love in the Want Ads

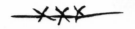

I remember the day I screwed up my courage to put in a personal ad. Filled with purpose, determined to meet the man of my dreams through this most literary of methods, I drove to the *Bay Guardian* office and, cringing, dictated my lines to a plump, impassive woman.

I half-expected her to arch an eyebrow at the obvious fabrications in the description of myself I gave her, and then, throwing a motherly arm across my shoulders, to step into a spotlight to belt out, "You Can't Hurry Love."

But she didn't. I slunk out, and three weeks later a brown packet came in the mail. I stole out to the deck with it like a dog sneaking a treat off the table, and spilled the letters and pictures out.

Whoa, *men city.* They were posing stiffly in front of bookshelves, beaming next to their cars. One had an arm around someone who had been ripped out of the picture. They wrote on flowered paper, on binder paper with ragged edges, on the backs of their electric bills.

In the end I answered three. One said he would know all he needed to know just by the sound of my voice, and I guess he did, because he never called me back. The second guy called me, although my note specially called for a written reply. "I found your name in the telephone book," he said in a deep, manly voice. "I hope I haven't overstepped my bounds."

Well, he had, but it was a nice voice. Impulsively, I asked him to come to dinner two days later. That would give me time, I figured, to lose ten pounds, get a tan and steam-clean the floors.

When the day came, I opened the door and there stood Alan. He was clutching a handful of daisies, still wet with rain. They looked an awful lot like the ones in my front garden.

"Hi, Alan, come in." I smiled and stood aside.

"Hey, I like your place!" Alan shouted. "Mind if I have a look around?"

Since I lived in a studio, I could hardly stop him. As Alan was poking his head into the bathroom and yelling that this was his first date in fourteen years, I decided that if I could just get Alan out of my apartment, I would never, never place another personal ad. From now on, I would let romance surprise me.

A couple of weeks later, one more letter arrived. This guy, Terry, didn't bother to include a picture. He just compared himself, point by point, to God.

Terry worked hard every day, whereas God had worked only six days in his life—"and part of that was spent on coming up with the appendix and New Jersey." Terry had lived all his adult life in the East Bay, whereas God could at best be described as a drifter. "Face it," Terry said. "The guy is all over the place."

We met at a department store. (I had learned my lesson.) After a little romance, we settled down to become friends. He isn't perfect—he doesn't think white folks should attempt dancing, can't pass a self-storage bin without wanting to lock himself in it for the weekend, and tends to drive great distances in the wrong direction, especially when you're trying to get someplace on time.

But he's always Terry, and I sure don't think I would have ever found him on my own. I bet Alan eventually found himself somebody, too, although it seemed to me he really wanted an apartment.

Life Is Over; Pass the Asp

The approach of Valentine's Day always brings up tender thoughts of "going" and "dumping" (going steady and breaking up). At Morgan and Patrick's middle school, you go with someone for some length of time—anywhere from two minutes to about a week—then you dump him or her.

It's a straightforward kind of thing. A kid comes up to a girl in the hall and says, "I hear Joel's going to dump you at lunch." The girl consults hurriedly with her friends, and dumps Joel at the mid-morning break. The dumping is done coldly, usually via a third party. "Lily says she doesn't want to go with you anymore." Or, simply and eloquently, "You're dumped."

When Larry Gallagher broke up with me back at the end of the eighth grade, he didn't say anything about how it was really his fault, that I was wonderful and deserved better, he just needed more space.

Instead he plucked meanly at the pitiful three rollers in my hair, which I was trying to fluff up after a radical Sassoon haircut. "Your hair looks stupid now," he said. "I don't want to go with you anymore."

Being a grown-up makes me nostalgic for these abrupt transitions. When I was going through another of those sensitive, protracted breakups myself, one where we both felt terrible because we couldn't make it work even though we were a thousand miles apart on every issue including how to hang the toilet paper, I used to envy my friend Peggy and her husband, Joe.

Her way of saying that she was annoyed and wanted to talk was to dump his clothes and fishing gear out the window and change the locks. Joe's way of replying, "I hear you, I value what you're saying, but I have my own point of view," was to stuff her favorite dress down the garbage disposal. She'd let some time go by, so he knew he was being heard, then she'd put Tide in his motor-cycle tank. When they were both winded, they'd talk, and it would either work out or she'd go back to her mother's.

When the rest of us mature grown-ups leave each other, though, we usually do it with brutal tact and sensitivity, dragging out the process inch by painful inch.

When my friend Roy was dumped by his girlfriend, she told him, "You're the nicest guy I've ever known. I just need more space." She held his hand when he cried. She cried herself. She took him to their favorite restaurant and said she'd miss all the jokes they shared, wrote him long letters explaining her motives. She awed him with how sensitively she was showing him the door, bludgeoned him with what a heart-stopping human being he was losing.

The temptation to be seen as wonderful even as one is departing often overrides the temptation to let someone down easy. A truly kind Caitlin might have yielded to old-fashioned impulse and tossed his gear out the window—in his case, unfortunately, camera equipment—and changed the locks.

If she had truly wanted Roy to get over her quickly, she would have thrown things, arrived for the last dinner late and looking haggard, sent her salmon back three times, talked too loudly, left lipstick on the napkin, whined about her job and told him she had always, always hated that jacket.

Instead of spending months grieving and going out of his way to walk by her house, Roy would have breathed an inward sigh of relief, thinking how close he came to marrying this raised-by-wolves creature. He would have been grateful to her, as I was to Larry, who so gallantly showed me his worst side as he was leaving, and let my heart go free.

Wasting Precious Mate-Hunting Time

Barbara De Angelis (author of *Secrets About Men Every Woman Should Know*) advises people to ask a new love interest questions about his relationship history on the first date, to make sure he's learned from his mistakes. "What else is significant to talk about," she said, "What movies they like? I mean, this will not tell you what kind of mate he or she is going to be."

Your date can't manage, on that first date, to tell you a little thing like why his last marriage went belly up? He or she seems uncomfortable being grilled? De Angelis says, "You have just received a wonderful warning that this person is not comfortable with disclosure and intimacy."

Bill and I must have done everything wrong, because it took us weeks to get to our respective relationship histories. On our first date, we went to a little waterfront place, and he bought me a glass of red wine. He told me a funny story about his car once flooding with rainwater, that he lived in a cottage on Russian Hill, that he had a weakness for denim skirts. We looked out the window at the ships moored there, and he told me about once when he was in the Navy he saw a black and white rainbow after a squall one moonlit night at sea.

I told him I had two kids, that I hardly ever wore skirts, that I would like another glass of wine.

We did establish that neither of us was married, but neither of us felt that this called for an explanation. All that came later, after we had wasted several weeks of potential mate-hunting time simply enjoying each other's company.

In time Bill and I learned the bitter truth: neither of us was a good candidate for marriage. When the time came to talk over our single days, like two weary old generals who had been on opposite sides, we were appalled at each other's pasts. As far as Bill could tell, I had made it a point to go out with men he found irritating, just from their descriptions. As far as I could tell—well, never mind. By the time we had finished talking about movies and the Navy and other irrelevant subjects, it was too late: we were hooked.

It doesn't seem all that easy to heed warnings, anyway. It's true I have met some stalwart, mature types who have: A friend of mine broke up with his girlfriend when she said she never wanted children. A woman stopped seeing a film producer she liked when he confessed his dream was to move to Boulder, Colorado, and sell gourmet goat cheese.

I remember both of these because I was surprised to find anybody had this strength of character. The rest of us, I suspect, who can't say no to an Oreo or a stupid sit-com or even one more trip down the water slide, are not going to stop seeing somebody who makes our socks slide into our shoes just because we discover some little thing like they're twelve light years from having even a minimal relationship. We're sure love will find a way. Once a man I was involved with forced me to read a letter his ex-wife had written to him, cataloging his sins. "It's all true, what she says here," he told me. I read it.

Well, sure, I thought to myself, briskly folding up the letter and putting it aside. That's how he behaved with *her*.

He, a man who lined up the pot handles on his way past the stove, had been over to my place, seen my kids flinging Cheerios and then me walking on the scattered cereal, and didn't hesitate for a minute when we decided to get a house together.

Because that's how it goes. The red flag goes up, and the speeding roadster tears madly, desperately, gladly right on past: Such is romance.

The Saying Is in the Doing

When Bill arrived at my house for the second time, back in November 1990, he had a wooden toilet lid over his shoulder. I hadn't even noticed that the toilet was broken. He knelt on the bathroom floor in his pressed slacks and fixed it, just like that.

Bill was able to tell me how he felt in words, too, but he didn't have to: I have noticed before how men talk when they're in love. They go around fixing things. They put up bookshelves, contribute to the grocery money, take your car in to see what's making that clicking sound, go over your presentation for you and offer advice.

When I noticed I was falling for Bill, I didn't prowl through his cottage looking for things to fix. I never once offered to take his car in for him or asked for a fork to see if I could get the toaster to work right.

Yet he never complained. He seemed to know that women have a different language for expressing love (that is, *language*)—that if I couldn't say it with a screwdriver then I could at least say it with words.

There are women reading this whose husbands have never said, "I love you"—or not in so many words. Girlfriends who wince when Valentine's Day or an anniversary rolls around, bringing no card, no flowers. It wounds them so, this neglect, that they don't notice that he finally got those blinds up on the back porch and got the CD player to stop sticking.

Many men use talk to solve problems, not to express feelings they think must be obvious. For them, love is doing. Carol Tavris, author of an excellent book called *The Mismeasure of Women*, says a friend of hers told her boyfriend, "Herb, I don't want you to do the male thing right now. I don't need advice. I've had a bad day, and I just want you to hold me and console me."

He looked absolutely perplexed. "What good will that do?" he asked.

Tavris points out what should be obvious: There is no difference between what men and women feel and how deeply they feel—only in how they express themselves. Women have been brought up to express emotion, men to suppress it. Men feel pressure at work to be stoic and pressure at home to express their feelings: We don't want a firefighter to burst into tears at the sight of a burning building, but when he comes home we want him to pour out his hopes and fears.

The stereotype of Woman as Intimacy Expert, Tavris says, is part of the insidious new Woman-Are-Better movement. The movement says men can't share and have superficial friendships based on a shared interest in the 49ers and Michelle Pfeiffer, while women are emotionally honest and mutually supportive. The philosophy behind the glut of "women are good, men are bad" books and articles is to teach women how to change their men to be more like women, the patently superior sex.

I don't know about this. I seem to remember someone telling me, long ago, about another patently superior sex. I didn't believe that, and I don't see why I should believe this.

Sure, there's room for improvement. It wouldn't kill you guys not to save up your explosions of joy and grief for the big game. If she needs to hear it in words, why not say it in words? Words are good for fixing things, too. I liked my new toilet lid a lot, but it isn't the kind of thing a girl can write down in her diary, now, is it?

But if men could benefit from expressing their feelings more easily, so could women benefit from learning to shut up about them once in a while and just get on with things. Instead of trying to turn them into our girl-friends, we could listen to the language men speak, in all the things they do.

But—Does Bill Know?

So the main squeeze and I went house hunting on Saturday . . .

Editor: Wait! What do you mean, you're house hunting with the main squeeze? Who is this guy? Did I miss something while I was out of town? You can't just hit people with this out of the blue.

OK, quick update on That Bill, as he tells me he is now known ("Oh, you're *that* Bill"). We met in the elevator at work three months ago. I noticed this guy out of the corner of my eye—tall, easy on the eyes—leafing through a stack of newspapers. He got on the elevator and said his happiness depended on knowing my name.

OK, OK, I asked him whether he worked in the building. I wasn't flirting. It was just important to me to know, just at that moment, who worked in the building and who didn't.

I administered the standard test—took him to a waterfront dive and ordered the house red. He didn't flinch. Furthermore, he has assured me I am the first woman he has ever been with—he and his first wife were just friends.

Moved by the frankness of this disclosure, and keeping in mind it was made by a fellow Irishman, I have let him in on a secret about my two room-mates, the short ones who pay no rent and fling bits of rolled-up clay out of slingshots at the kitchen windows. "They call me Mom," I told him, "out of affection and old habit. Actually, we're just friends."

Fade to: calendar with pages ripping off. Thanksgiving goes by, the holidays, the New Year. We meet each other's families.

My mother thinks Bill's funny—and she's the one who usually starts liking my boyfriends about two years after we've broken up ("Where's Ted?" she'll ask about the man she encouraged to wait out in the car. "I always liked him"). My sisters make it a point of liking my boyfriends, even the ones they can't stand, but they seemed to like this one especially. His parents are so great it's as if they were sent over by Central Casting.

After that it kind of snowballed on us. Two weeks ago, Bill expertly lit a Presto log in his fireplace ("Most people," he explained with obvious pride, "would light it at just one end. Big mistake"), poured a spunky Napa red into two glasses, and asked me whether I would—I can still hardly get my fingers to type the words—*marry* him.

It took me an hour to stammer out an answer, but I said I would. Gladly.

I told the kids one by one. Patrick said, "I like Bill a lot. I guess it would be all right."

Then he bounced the basketball for a minute and said, "Does Bill know?"

Morgan was next. At first she didn't believe me and Patrick—she had to call Bill up. Then she said, "This is so great. Can I invite my friends to the party? Can I drink champagne? What are you going to *wear?*"

I said I didn't know. Before we can set a date and plan the bash, we have to figure out where we're all going to hang our toothbrushes.

So that's how we came to find ourselves, a couple of innocents wandering hand in hand, followed by two skeptical preadolescents wearing Walkmans, through the dark, murky Slough of Despond that is the Bay Area housing market.

On Thursday: A hardworking professional couple, both thirty-nine, with two incomes (but no down payment to speak of), amuse the real estate agents and the relatives as they try to find a $300,000 house with three bedrooms and two bathrooms without moving to Manteca.

Suburban Dreams and Linoleum Horrors

Bill and I were on the Bay Bridge, arguing, in that elaborately polite way you do in these early stages, about whether to rent or to buy.

I pointed out that with our two incomes, we could rent a wonderful three-bedroom city flat for us and the kids.

Picture it, I said. These days you can rent a lot more house than you can buy. While homeowners stayed home, watching the cracks spreading along the foundation, we'd throw parties in our spacious sunny flat, stretching out an idle hand to call the landlord if we should notice a lightbulb dimming.

Bill smiled. "We're both nearly forty," he said (rather unkindly, I thought), "yet we're still ending every year with a pile of rent receipts and nothing else, still getting clobbered by taxes, still looking through other people's windows."

"Besides," I went on as if no one had spoken, "buying a house is supposed to be the biggest transaction of a person's life. It takes financial wizardry. We're former English majors who can't play a jukebox without losing the quarter."

I unleashed my big point. The market is very uncertain, I said, even for people who have some remote idea of what they're doing. Everybody who bought houses last year, before prices began to drop, is standing on his porch, reading the business page and weeping.

"But even we can see that means it's a buyer's market," Bill countered. By now we were on I–80, with the skyline of the city we love receding behind us. "When we're a couple of geezers counting pennies, we might be glad we bought that overpriced stucco horror in a dreary little suburb back in '91."

Then we just drove. We were starting our search in Albany because it has a school district to die for. Bill was hoping, I knew, that the sight of white picket fences, curtains and neat green lawns would stir something atavistic in my soul, making me long for a driveway and an easement and a debt ratio I could call my own.

I was sure, for my part, that having a little gander at what was available in our price range would send this city man scurrying back over the bridge, a confirmed renter.

We looked at houses all afternoon. The agent, working with the figures we gave her, showed us postage-stamp back yards jammed up against used-car lots, pastel green bedrooms, pink rugs.

We turned on faucets, mentally stripped off wallpaper and carted away geegaws. We did some depressing arithmetic that showed that even the meanest of these hovels would stretch our monthly income to the limit.

Bill went completely silent about the time the agent showed us Motel Six, the low-ceilinged, linoleum horror advertised as three bedrooms and a spa. We were both shaken. We wondered what we had done, after working hard at our careers—after working hard to find each other—to have to commute over a clogged bridge to a tiny suburb in the East Bay flats.

When did the American Dream become such a nightmare?

Like thousands before us and thousands after us, we face some hard choices. Should we try to scrape up a down payment and buy this spring, before prices go up? Wait? Or forget the whole thing, rent a flat, throw a big Irish bash, and go to Paris on our honeymoon? Should we build equity or memories?

An Offer No One Can Accept

"Are you *sure* there's no chance of their accepting this offer?" I asked Janice again.

"Well, they could," Janice, our real estate agent, said in the cool, somewhat distracted way that charmed us from the first. She forgets phone numbers and gets addresses wrong and once took us at night to see a house where the electricity had been shut off (too dark, we decided)—all of which reassures us that she is our kind of person.

After four weeks of house-hunting, Bill and I found a small house we liked in the less-fashionable west end of Noe Valley in San Francisco.

Built in 1906, it's covered with peeling gray stucco, has three bedrooms, a garage, and an enthusiastic rock fan next door. Janice kept apologizing for it, and trying to get us back in the car, but we were impulsive first-time buyers, already slapping our pockets for the checkbook.

The owner must be in despair. He has had it on the market since May, and has dropped his asking price twice, the last time, as both the Gulf War and the recession were heating up, to a panicky $329,000.

All without getting a single nibble, in open house after open house. Then we come along, with an offer only a lunatic would accept.

We wanted the place, but not so badly that we wanted the owner to actually sell it to us. This is all just for fun, right? We aren't really going to get hundreds of thousands of dollars in debt, are we?

A very sweet savings and loan guy came over to our house and gave us the lowdown: "The market will definitely go up, or it will definitely go down, or it will definitely freeze where it is right now," he said over a bottle of Red Tail ale. "I'm not sure *I'd* know a good deal right now."

So we wanted to build a dip in the market into our cheesy offer.

"Offer them $285,000," Bill suggested to Janice as the three of us sat around my kitchen table. "OK," she said. I had the feeling Janice would say OK if we suggested the owner stop being piggish and simply *give* us the house.

"How about the closing costs?" she asked. Closing costs would be seven or eight grand. "Oh, well, I think he should pay those, don't you?" I was half joking, but Janice said, "OK."

We tried to think of some other things we could make the sellers do. Pay for the termite inspection? Throw in the washer and dryer? Come up on the weekends and do our laundry?

I hate to take advantage of a poor strapped seller in a plummeting market who will make only 80 grand or so on this deal, but it has been a long time in California since the groveling landless (but employed) poor had any power.

So we are also putting a measly $15,000 down (all the money we have in the world), and asking the owner to lend us 15 percent of the rest.

I was still fretting that the owner might go for it. "Can we make the offer subject to the approval of our attorney?" I asked. "Sure," said Janice, and wrote that in. The lawyer we have in mind is my laid-back friend Zimmie, who might help us slither out of a deal if we promised to stop talking about marriage in front of his girlfriend.

We sent the offer over, and instead of saying, "Oh, grow up," and ripping it into a million pieces, as any lucid person would have done, he accepted our preposterous terms. But he wanted $325,000, and for us to do our own stupid laundry, and to pay half the closing costs.

Hell. We'll rent.

When Your Mate Just Doesn't Match

Many of you out there are too evolved to care what your mate wears. I envy you that, because if Bill wore a suit to a family bash or jeans to the theater I would be embarrassed. People would assume this was the most I could attract, a guy who wears Levi's to see *Lear.*

Besides, then he wouldn't match me. "A mate is, among other things, an accessory," a friend says. "Like a handbag." She says that when they're getting ready to go out, her own husband will wander into the kitchen and say, "Is this all right?" She'll stare at his jeans and T-shirt and say, slowly, "I'm wearing a cocktail dress. We're going to a cocktail party. Do you think we look as if we match?"

At our house, admittedly, I'm the problem. On a typical evening Bill has to complete his outfit—blazer, slacks, very fly tie—with his usual accessory, a woman covered with corn flakes and lint, the back of her hair not combed because she can't see back there, vagabond mascara under her eyes, wearing black jeans and a sweater.

He can't go out with a thing like that on his arm. Someone is bound to see him. Oh, they'll say to themselves, what a fabulous tie, but my God, that wife. She doesn't go at all.

The problem facing so many of us is how to get our accessories to wear something else. You can simply say, "Is that what you're going to wear?" but this doesn't always work. Bill says this, and I say, "Yes, why?" I am reading a magazine, ready to go, happy with the way the jeans match the black stripe in my sweater. I may echo that black again in my earrings.

What can he do with me? His friends will feel a momentary thrill of well-being, knowing their own wives are looking sharp, man. And Bill and I will look as if we got dressed on opposite sides of the planet.

Clothes are important to all of us. They convey messages about our money, our status, our taste. It's nuts, but it's true. Statistics show that 96 percent of women look first at a man's clothes, then at his face. Men are so cowed by the idea of looking wrong they've invented a global uniform—baggy dark suit, white shirt, shoes like black pecan shells. At summit conferences, male world leaders look as if they called each other up and said, "What are you wearing? The dark suit and the white shirt? What for shoes? Black? OK, see you there."

I've been talking to my friends about how they steer their disheveled mates into better sartorial choices. My friend Mary picks out her boyfriend's clothes, and he wears them. He'll wear whatever's on top of the pile. "If a tutu were on top, he'd wear that," she says. Once—this is true—a car came speeding down their alley and a suitcase fell out. It held three Brooks Brothers suits, exactly his size.

Not everybody can wait for this to happen. The one of you who doesn't care about this should defer to the one who does. If that doesn't happen, sometimes you just have to pull a gun on them and take them shopping. That's how I got my green suit, anyway—Bill dragged me into a store and made me buy it.

He was right, too. We were almost ready to go the other night when I noticed him looking at me. "What?" I said.

"Nothing, you look great. I was just thinking how sensational you always look in your green suit," he said.

I put it on. I know he wouldn't steer his own accessory wrong.

Same Flat, New Boyfriend

Friends seemed surprised when I told them that the flat Bill and I and the kids are moving to is the one I lived in three years ago, with Nick.

That's not so odd—that place simply happened to come back on the rental market just when I was combing the ads for a large flat in Noe Valley. Bill liked it—high ceilings, lots of rooms—but said, as he handed me the pen to sign the lease, "Are you sure it won't bother you to go back and be reminded of all that?"

Thumb backward through the calendar to a summer night several years ago, when Nick and I signed that same lease. He lived in the flat next to mine, and we decided, in the way you do, that if side-by-side living was blissful we should immediately change it and do something else, like move in together.

It wasn't as if I didn't know that Nick was neat. Whenever I dropped my purse onto his couch he picked it up and stowed it by the door. I'd be trailing perfume down his hall, batting my eyes and lingering seductively by the heating vent, and he'd be wondering where I might have put my wine glass down, and how he could unobtrusively retrieve it and wash it.

But I have always wanted to be neater, and his ex-wife had convinced him that he could stand to be a little more relaxed around the house. We'd be good for each other.

Nice plan.

We moved in on a sunny day in July, and after five months together that would make a terrific Brian de Palma movie, we agreed to live apart in the same house, Man Who Aligns Pot Handles and his little girl downstairs, and Woman Who Litters Floor With Rubber Bands and Puts Dishes Away While Still Wet huddled upstairs with her Cheerios-lobbing offspring.

I know I am being peculiar again, but it doesn't bother me to remember those months.

It's true that I would just as soon forget the time I tossed Nick's all-cotton dress shirts in the dryer and he wasn't a bit understanding about it, or the way he fussed at little things like a butter knife stuck with honey in his silverware drawer.

But then I'd have to lose, too, my memory of the time I went to his company party and he let me throw away my shoes, and the Friday nights we went out, losing to all comers at shuffleboard and dancing until his jeans were dark with sweat.

I'd lose the time I spent on his five-year-old daughter's bed, sipping wine and watching a 500-act play that she made up as she went along.

Look at me. I made a horrible mistake and here I am waxing nostalgic about it.

I know it's odd, but I feel a lingering warmth for anybody I was ever close to—for anyone who ever shared with me his childhood fears, his secrets, his life, even his views on how Teflon pans can poison you. I don't want to forget it ever happened.

My dad says it's a mistake to willingly expunge any part of your life—that the worst parts are vital ingredients for the best.

Part of this is, of course, that you can take valuable lessons away from every disaster: For example, the last thing I would do, as I lower my pen to sign the identical lease for the identical flat, is to move in with another neat guy.

One who refolds kitchen rags I have already crumpled into a perfectly acceptable shape, or whose cottage was actually photographed for a book, or who can be so orderly he can remind himself of something he wants to do just by putting his keys down in a new place.

Move in with someone like this again?

That would be silly.

Being There, Without Reservations

As some of you will remember, back in March Bill and I had been talking about whether to rent a flat and honeymoon in Paris this summer or to do something depressingly sensible, such as buy a house that will support us in our old age.

We rented, of course, and now we're off to London next week, then Paris, while the kids go to South Dakota with their dad. We're not married yet, but we don't see why we should let that get in the way of a honeymoon.

There we'll be drinking Pernod in a Parisian cafe, watching the crowd go by and wondering where we're going to sleep that night because neither of us got around to making reservations.

Bill and I have discovered that we are perfectly suited to each other. His idea of planning a trip is the same as mine: Do nothing and hope that the other person will eventually panic and start making some calls.

I don't mean to say that we did nothing to prepare. Starting months ago, not a day has passed when one or the other of us didn't come home with a stack of books: French novels, histories, walking tours of London, the Pax Britannica trilogy, *A Moveable Feast*, *A Tale of Two Cities*, *Les Miserables*, a smattering of Balzac, some restaurant guides.

It was inspirational, the way we plunged into our preparations. I sat puzzling over *Madame Bovary* with the help of three dictionaries, and Bill lounged next to me reading a biography of George Sand. We read aloud to each other on our weekend outings, and Bill took to calling me his little cabbage. Not wanting to overlook anything that might prove important, we even rented French movies: *Camille Claudel, Au Revoir les Enfants, Murmur of the Heart.*

It seemed to us that we were ready. So it came as a jolt, as July neared, to remember we didn't have plane tickets.

For a long while, it was a standoff: Bill would linger over the newspaper ads, calling my attention to the pictures of airplanes, and I would again mention to him the name of a travel agency that, I was pretty sure, could get us on one.

Finally one morning, in a burst of energy, I called my travel agent, Kevin, and gave him our travel dates and my Visa number. I put down the phone, exhausted, but feeling all the exhilaration of an unpleasant task squarely faced.

I coasted on the feeling for days.

With the trip planned, we both felt better. We went back to our books, now piled three and four deep on the coffee table, and the days passed in a pleasant blur. Occasionally one of us would remark that it would be nice to have somewhere to stay when the plane landed in London. Once we glanced through a book called *Cheap Sleeps in London* and had to smile at the prices. Oh, that dry English wit.

One day in late June, I pointed out to Bill that having reservations tended to take the fun out of it anyway. Why go at all if we knew exactly what was going to happen to us when we got there? After I said that, for some reason, he seemed nervous. He added *Cheap Sleeps in Paris* to our pile, putting it down on the kitchen table right where my cereal bowl usually goes.

I gave in, and got us a room at L'Ermitage, in Montmartre, for 380 francs a night. I'm sure that's cheap—they said it was a long uphill climb from the Metro—but I don't know because it was Bill's job to figure out how much that is in dollars, and he's had his hands full boning up on the French Revolution.

Wish us *bonne chance.*

Reno Beckons, Reality Intrudes

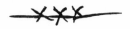

Nobody believes us anymore when Bill and I give them a wedding date. "We're getting married in November," we tell them. "Sure you are," they answer, not writing it down.

When Bill proposed in January, we planned to get married right away. I believe that if a thing is to be done well it should be done impulsively and without planning.

All we had to do is work out a few details. How many people? Rings? Vows? A band? Could single people bring dates? Do we register? Will he take my name or should I take his or should we get a new name? Where should we have the wedding?

Friends and relatives were helpful. "I hope you're not getting married in some damned redwood grove," Bill's friend Mike told him. My mother suggested we get married at the community center in her very nice mobile home park, which has a view of the duck pond and besides would cut down on her driving.

"No way am I getting married in a trailer park," Bill said, not realizing that for me it would be a step up. My family tradition, going strong now for three generations, calls for a short, romantic sprint to Reno.

I told Bill about the wonderful time I had going to Reno with one of my sisters a couple years ago. I described the champagne, her constant smile, her new husband's unpredictable dive-bombing hugs, the joy we all felt in that tacky pink chapel. "They were so happy," I say, remembering. "But that's so sad," Bill answered, shuddering. He doesn't understand.

He wants it to be nice, and he wants his whole world there, from his parents to the editorial assistants right down to everybody who has ever smiled at him.

In fact, his idea of pruning his list, just so you know what I'm up against, is to come into the room and tell me that I'm forcing him to cut dozens of his closest friends, and how hurt they'll be when they find out. Then he examines his list again and says, about a good friend of his that I've met exactly twice, "You know, Kate is really more your friend than mine. I really think she should be on your list."

We have to agree on the invitations, the ceremony, the clothes, the music and the flowers. Bill asks if we should get somebody to decorate the room, and suddenly it's too much: I freeze, scared of the fuss, the expense, the formality. He sees my face and his own face falls. We stand there unhappily, confused by our own unhappiness: Why have a wedding at all, if it costs too much and causes fights and scares the bejesus out of you besides?

Bill knows why, and, in my rare moments free from panic, I do, too.

Even if your twelve-year-old daughter finishes off the champagne and barfs in the potted palm, as Morgan is planning to do, and you flub your lines, and the cake melts and the band never shows but your wreck of a dad does, stepping into the reception line more or less over your mother's dead body—even if your dress is all wrong and nobody ever got the coffee machine working and the whole thing goes so fast you don't get a chance to talk to half the people: Even then, getting married is what you do if you fall in love and you want to do something really drastic about it.

Something right out in front of everybody, so you know, and he knows, and they know, that you both agree you have, after all, something worth celebrating, something worth making a fuss about.

Embarking upon the Streetcar of Love

On Saturday morning, several hours before I was due to get married, I kept squinting at my hair, which the girls at the shop had insisted on curling. I wasn't nervous. I was just worried that I had got too little sleep, and thought I was getting cramps, and I definitely had high hair. Bill was going to be marrying Edith Bunker.

He had gone hiking with his friend Tom. This is good, I thought, a trifle crankily, a little solitude for me in these last hours.

I washed out my new hairdo in the sink and felt a little better.

Then I just sat on the couch.

Marriage.

We had met one year ago to the day. I walked up the street with him, exchanging small talk, thinking secretly anybody that good-looking had to be gay.

For weeks I kept kicking his tires, but he just went on turning up, bringing me a new toilet lid, fixing the faucet, charming the kids. He took the best side of the bed, like a man, but explained it was so he could keep his sword arm free in case he needed to defend me in the night.

This had been a long time coming, for both of us. We have agreed we couldn't have made this work in our twenties, even with each other.

My dad calls it streetcar love, saying that you ride along with someone for as long as he's going the same way you are, then you find someone else who is going your way for the next leg of the journey.

"While two people may get on within a short distance of each other," he said, "they never get off at the same stop, for the simple reason that no two people have exactly the same destination. If they exit together then the sacrifice of one destroys the hope of another."

He's right, but who said anything about getting off? The idea here is to go to the end of the line this time.

The wedding that night, at the very cool South of Market loft of our friend Kate Beckwith, was like a dream sequence out of "This Is Your Life." Morgan stood beside me with flowers in her hair. Patrick stood next to her in his first suit. My twin, Adrian, was there, looking a little better than was strictly necessary, considering that I was the bride.

I only fidgeted a little bit, holding a gorgeous bouquet made by my friends Ray and Bob, hiding a grease mark that had leaped onto my skirt as I walked in and wondering why my groom had to stand quite so far away, especially as he was looking at me in that way I particularly liked. Bill's brother Rich was best man, friends recited frankly wonderful passages from things, and the kids gave me away.

Everybody started dancing so fast that I never got to remove my garter to the music of "Love Potion No. 9," as arranged, and now I never will because the ball and chain says he's sorry but this is it, neither of us is getting married again, ever.

How good are our chances? Fifty percent of all marriages fail, statistics say.

Today, I am inclined to turn that statistic around: Fifty percent of all marriages succeed. Fully half of those couples you see smiling at each other at the altar will stay together until death does them part.

The kids helped us open the presents, which was difficult for them, because none was for them.

One was a magnum of red wine from our friend Brian, with a note: "This is good now, but will improve with time, like your marriage."

Love Has Appetizers
Before Main Course

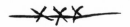

The married couple had some people over for dinner the other night, a friend and her new boyfriend.

The courting pair seemed very fond of each other, often breaking off in conversation to kiss, or embrace. By dessert they were holding hands under the table and looking at their watches.

The married couple clinked their forks, and drank their wine, and talked about movies, but they had the feeling they were keeping the other couple from something, if you know what I mean.

There the wife was, brilliantly analyzing *Cliffhanger* and they were looking at her with what they clearly hoped was a rapt expression, while all the time imagining each other naked in whichever of the bedrooms was nearest.

Refusing all offers of coffee and mumbling lies about work in the morning, they made their disgracefully hasty exit at 9:45.

For every married couple who has ever invited such a pair into their home, the comparison is there for anybody to make: their level of romance and yours. Their sex life and yours.

Left alone, the married couple cleans the kitchen. She rinses the dishes while he wraps up the remains of the roast chicken. They both know that the other couple are off somewhere in the city, removing each other's clothes with their teeth.

When the kitchen is clean, the married couple gets ready for bed. He tries to get the cat to come in; she brushes her teeth. "Cute butt, mister," she mutters as she passes him to take the dog out for a pee. "Keep your eyes to yourself, lady," he answers, giving up on the cat and taking the garbage out.

Not much romance going on here. She knows him pretty well now, this human being raised eating different cereal in a different town, whose enthusiasms and tastes and ordinary stubbornnesses were formed long before she came along, with her quite different tastes and stubbornnesses.

She knows his biggest dilemma is to figure out which side of the bed he likes more so he can hog it. She's resigned to his opening windows just before he goes to work and getting upset about a little thing like the dog chewing up the sunglasses he left on the bed.

He knows her, too. There she is every morning, reading funny bits of the paper aloud to him while he's trying to read the sports. When they go out for coffee she will say she doesn't want a pineapple muffin, then will stare fixedly at his until he gives her a bite. He knows she has abandoned her early pretense of being a maniac for fresh air and is "studying" the new fall TV shows. Sometimes she absentmindedly opens and drinks the wine he was saving.

He knows when they go to bed, warm back to warm back, the cat will yowl outside the window, and she'll feign sleep.

Meanwhile, the courting couple, their passion spent, lie awake, side by side, staring into the darkness.

She's trying to get over the ducks on his shower curtain, and he's wondering if sitting cross-legged on the bed while flossing her teeth is a regular nightly routine for her.

Of course, a lot of discoveries still lie ahead of them. She doesn't know yet that he feels better when all the pot handles are facing the same way, and is not exactly divorced. He doesn't know she'll look at the rock formations that excite him and say, "They're just rocks, OK? I'm going back to the car."

The married couple, miles across the city, go to sleep almost immediately.

When he turns over, so does she, automatically.

They are awakened minutes later by a strangled yowl from outside the window. The wife doesn't stir.

"Hell," says the husband.

Can Bonding Save This Relationship?

It was almost a year ago. Patrick and I were walking over to the basketball court to shoot some hoops. "Remember when you asked me if I was going to marry Bill?" I said. "Well, I might."

He thought about that. "I guess it would be all right," he said. "I like Bill a lot. But . . ."

"But what?"

"There's this kid at school who said he really liked his mom's boyfriend until they got married, and then the boyfriend got really mean and started bossing the kid around. He even bossed the mom around."

"That does happen," I agreed. "It happens a lot. But I don't think it'll happen with Bill, do you?"

"No," he said.

I reported to Bill that it was as we had suspected: the kid would shape up. He just needed firm handling.

Now when Bill opens the front door at night, wanting only to take off his tie and relax, Patrick is there yelling insults at him down the stairwell. Bill ignores him as he kisses me, then says to me, loudly, "Your son seems to be in a tearing hurry to get his butt whipped."

"Oh yeah?" says Patrick. "Come and get me, buttface."

An hour later I trip over the two of them in the hallway, panting on the rug after the wrestling match, still weakly trading insults.

Morgan confers with Bill about his tie in the morning, tries her outfits on for him, teaches him to say, "That's really ill" when he likes something.

I'm not worried about those three. The problem is something entirely more serious.

It's the stepcat.

When, at first, Bill didn't seem especially eager to pick Mike up and pet him, I figured he was taking his time, as he did so instinctively with the kids. His habit of going out of his way to kick Mike out of the bedroom was, I was sure, a way of not smothering him with too much affection too soon.

But when this continued for over a year, I realized that the two of them were still bogged down in that oedipal conflict, cat versus boyfriend. Turning to my stepparenting book for ideas on helping them get closer, I suggested to Bill that he and Mike could cement their bond by doing things together.

Bill picked Mike up, gave him a perfunctory pat, and dumped him out the back door.

"That isn't what I meant," I said.

"Dumb cat," Bill said.

It would be hard to argue that someone who spends all afternoon in the Brookstone bag is not dumb, but Mike has other qualities. "For example," I pointed out. "He guards the house."

And he does. He watches from the window all day, like a sentry. Burglars see him there. They head off down the block, one saying to the other, "It's no good, Al, they have a guard cat. Better find another house."

It's true that Mike makes mistakes that set the whole relationship back, like grooming himself on our bed in the middle of the night and shaking the whole bed. "Stop it," I hiss at him. "You look *fine.*" But he does it anyway.

The fleas he brought in during that October hot spell were probably not a good idea either, although you wouldn't think one tiny flea on his shirt cuff could upset a grown man that way. I set off hissing flea bombs in every room and got Mike a collar guaranteed to keep them on their side of the international dateline. Upset by the strength of the collar, Mike peed on Bill's stereo speaker. "That isn't like him," I told Bill as he silently mopped it up.

"Dumb cat," Bill said.

Back at the Beginning
Not a Bad Place to Be

I had finally found the number of John "The Careful Hauler," and he had come over to give us a bid. He moved Bill and me and the kids into this cavernous duplex on Church Street fifteen months ago.

If he was surprised that we were leaving Noe Valley again so soon, he didn't say so. He just said, "Where to this time?," as if I had called a cab.

"Well, back to Scott Street," I said. "Where you moved me from the last time." I lived then next door to the kids' dad, Jim, with only a wooden fence between his back yard and mine.

"Going back to the same exact place?" John asked, glancing at our stacks of boxes and making notes.

"Well, almost," I said. I didn't have the time it would take to explain that this time we are moving right into my ex-husband's Victorian. We didn't have the money to buy a whole house and didn't want to leave the city, so we are buying a flat from him.

Right under the one he lives in, actually. We'll be tenants in common, a term usually meaning that you own a building together, but in our case meaning I guess anything you'd like it to.

The kids will live under one roof with both parents again, something they haven't done since they were four and six. "You won't have half your stuff ten blocks away anymore," I told them one morning over dinner. "You'll have both Mom and Dad around all the time again."

The kids were not impressed. "All our friends live in Noe Valley," they grouched. They are wary of the idea of having both their parents around all the time, though they know other kids who have to put up with this. "You mean you see your mother every DAY?" I once overheard Morgan asking her friend Danielle.

And, of course, the family has grown. During her eight years of wandering the desert of the city, her Mom met and married a gentle Irishman, someone even an ex-husband could like, and tossed him into the equation.

You are probably thinking, gee, they seem so calm and civilized. But isn't that a little *close* when the ex-husband's floor is their ceiling? What are they, passionless, anemic, Russian?

It may not work. The kids may pine for Noe Valley. We may get into fistfights over whose turn it is to water the yard, seize familiar-looking vases from each other's flats, smash a lot of crockery and end up like characters in an O'Neill play.

Then again, maybe it will work. We'll meet each other's friends and throw house parties at which the guests will gather in the corners and gossip about our living arrangement.

The kids may discover they like having all their clothes, or even all their parents, in one place. Jim and I will be able to call Patrick's bluff when he says he left his math book over at Dad's, and we'll be in a better position to keep an eye on Morgan and help her at Lowell.

And, of course, Bill and I will get to own something (and finally shut up about real estate). Jim will get to sell something. But nothing, neither the money nor the flat, will actually leave the family.

I led John The Careful Hauler through the house. "Is this going?" he asked. He was pointing to a red couch, rather the worse for wear, that has accompanied me on my wanderings.

It belonged to the Scott Street house before any of the rest of us did: Jim found it stored in the basement of the Victorian years ago. "I guess so," I said.

That couch has been going around in circles for years. Time it settled down. Time I did, too.

When Your Spouse Knows You
Like a Book

Bill and I were setting out over the hill to 24th Street to have our coffee on Saturday morning. He had urged me to take my book, but I didn't want to lug it along.

Half an hour later we were there. We found a seat on the bench outside, then Bill said, "Do you want a muffin?" I said no, as I always do. "Are you absolutely sure?" he asked. With just a trace of irritation in my tone, I told him I was sure.

He cast a final doubtful glance at me, then went off to get our coffee. When he returned, he put his pineapple bran muffin on the bench on his other side, where I couldn't see it. We both settled down with our coffee and the paper.

As Bill started to eat his muffin, I kept looking over. I like the top best. He sighed and broke me off a piece of the top. "I thought you didn't *want* a muffin," he said.

"I didn't," I said, licking the crumbs off my fingers. The fact that I wanted a muffin now didn't have anything to do with what I may have said a few minutes ago. I am a woman of many moods.

A few minutes later I'd finished my sprint through the paper, eaves-dropped on the conversations around me and admired the violinist with Rastafarian hair and a pink miniskirt who was playing a mournful tune opposite us. I drummed my fingers on my knees.

"You wish you had brought your book, don't you?" Bill said. I admitted it.

"Here you go." He pulled my book out of his pocket. "I knew you'd want it. You always do, after you finish the paper."

I took the book somewhat frostily. Of course I appreciated it. It's sweet of him to know my habits so well. But I was not charmed at being accused, almost in so many words, of being predictable.

I want to be known, naturally. It's pleasant to have my needs anticipated, the way they do at a high-class hotel, where you find your hometown newspaper on your breakfast tray and the eggs cooked exactly three-and-a-half minutes, the way you like them.

But I don't want to be known in the sense that you think you know what I might do next.

My grandmother was outwardly a person of settled habits. She always wanted to go to the same seafood restaurant. She always ordered a Manhattan, and she always grilled the waitress about every item on the menu. Then she'd order the prawns.

Everybody else grew impatient, but for me there was true suspense in her order. In her mind, I could tell, she was the most reckless of gourmets, taking new risks at every meal. Her decision to go with the prawns was made anew each time, a surprise pick from a dazzling array of choices.

Like my grandmother, I am outwardly a person who will, every time, refuse to get her own muffin and then pick at her husband's. Inwardly, that's not who I am at all. Inwardly, I might skip the whole walk, loot my bank account and take the red eye to Rio. I might meet my deadline as usual, or I might throw over my job to become the resident goddess to a cranky but progressive tribe in Papua, New Guinea.

In a marriage, it's a good thing to anticipate your beloved's desires with the delicacy of a Swiss hotel manager, to be able to predict that she'll start yawning at a party at exactly 10:19, to know how many scoops of chocolate she takes in her loathsome brew of instant coffee, and when she needs a book to anchor her to the bench on Saturday mornings.

It's a good thing, too, to contrive always to be surprised and delighted by the other's choices. "Going to bed at ten and falling asleep over your book as usual? Oh, you madcap!"

"Let's walk back over Castro Street instead of Noe," I said to Bill when it was time to head back. "But you always . . ." he began, but then seeing my look, subsided. "Inspired idea," he said.

I really believe that's what drew him to me—that he just never knows what I'm going to do next.

The Cat Has to Go; Sure Thing

"I think an animal is the purest experience you can have," Audrey Hepburn once said. "They are totally dependent on you, and therefore totally vulnerable. And this complete vulnerability is what enables you to open up your heart completely, which you rarely do with a human being."

For a different view, we turn to a friend, John Smithyman, who has some advice for Bill, a man then about to move in with a cat.

"Cats are stupid. Once you let one move into your house, you will not be rid of it until it dies a messy and expensive death of old age."

John claims that his friend's cousin saw a study hushed up by the cat lobby and the NRA proving that most handgun deaths are caused by a guy coming home to find that the cat has peed on his shoes again.

Bill doesn't like cats. He used to send me cartoons of cat-free bookstores and recipes for kitty fritters and curried cat, and he would sometimes deposit Mike in the bathroom with a trifle more force than necessary.

I happen to like the little furniture-scratching machine myself. I think a cat makes a room look peaceful. Besides, pets are just plain nice. They bring out tenderness in us, and make us laugh, and give us an excuse to go to the park.

But they aren't up there with people. I like Mike, but I like Bill more. I know this is politically incorrect, but I put his happiness above Mike's. If he didn't like cats, perhaps it was time to find the cat a new home.

I couldn't just give him away, of course. The kids are devoted to him. "Isn't he just the best cat?" Patrick frequently says, hugging Mike so hard that Mike's eyes go lopsided. Patrick's attachment doesn't include doing anything to keep Mike from starving, of course, and Morgan has a way of wailing my name when the cat doodoos disturb her primping ritual in the bathroom, but they might take it hard if I just unloaded him. I still have some hard questions for my own parents about the mysterious disappearance of Ragmop, our poodle, when we moved to the house across from the high school.

So I mentioned to Bill that cats often get lost during a move.

"You could find him a good home, feign an exhaustive search, and nobody would know the difference," I said. "Just don't tell me anything about it." I was at least half-serious.

On moving day, though, I looked down at my ankles and discovered I still had a cat. I brought Mike over to his new house, and he roamed unhappily through the unfamiliar rooms, complaining at the top of his voice. Then the wind blew the front door open, and he darted through it, tire fodder on a rendezvous with destiny.

When I ran out the door to look for him, he was gone. This is precisely what I said happens on moves: Cat freaks out, leaves. Posters appear on lampposts, with dim Xeroxes showing cat as he looked when he was a kitten, telling where he was lost, offering a reward. Cat is never found.

I told Bill Mike was gone, and he shook his head, got his jacket, then disappeared out the door himself.

Fifteen minutes later he reappeared, with a sheepish Mike dangling from one arm. "Stupid cat," Bill muttered as he carried him into the house and carefully set him down.

Now I keep catching Bill freshening Mike's water. "Well, somebody has to do it," he growls when I raise an eyebrow.

"The little s— can stay as long as he doesn't mangle my couch," he says, reaching a hand down to stroke the purring cat in his lap.

Everybody Makes Mistakes

I am sitting in my back porch office, the radio blasting, the electric blanket warming my chair. Everything is as it should be, but I can't work.

I'm sick about Bill's shirt.

Ever since I wrecked two of his dress shirts by throwing them in the dryer, I've been as careful as I can. I would rather wash the clothes than do the cooking—Bill does that—and I like folding them and putting them in piles, thinking about my family the way my mother says she used to think about each of us as she pinned our clothes to the line.

Besides, I can't accept the idea that I can't even do the laundry right.

So as I put a load of shirts in the washer this morning, I said to myself: "Don't put these in the dryer, don't put these in the dryer." I left a hanger on top of the washer to remind myself.

And it worked. I noticed the hanger, and hung Bill's shirts to dry in the shower.

That's when I saw it: a huge new yellow stain flooding the collar and part of the front of his best shirt.

Where did it come from? I washed that white shirt with other white clothes. I was actually thinking about the wash as I did the wash.

On mornings like these, I resent having always to be trapped inside this idiot. Every day, from now until the end of my life, I have to go with her wherever she goes, to the kitchen to blow up a cup of coffee in the microwave, out to the streets to plow into a stranger's car while unwrapping a piece of gum, or down to the laundry room to destroy the ball and chain's wardrobe, shirt by shirt.

Some people with a determinedly cheerful outlook maintain there's some comfort in making mistakes. "If everything were to turn out just as I planned for it to," says author Hugh Prather, "then I would never experience anything new; my life would be an endless repetition of stale successes."

That's one fate I've been spared so far, those everlasting successes. Instead, I have to make all sorts of absurd allowances for myself. Anybody could repeatedly whack into the wall backing out of the garage. A statistically measurable number of people put the shampoo bottle back upside down with the cap off so it drips a blue trail down the wall.

Most drivers double-park with the engine running in rush hour, sprint in to drop off a video, then return to find the keys locked in the car.

I allow myself these ordinary mistakes. It's only when I'm genuinely trying, as now, to do the wash right that frustration sets in. I'd like to keep the fiction alive in my own mind that I don't do things right, not that I can't. I need to think of myself as a potentially perfect person, even if all evidence goes against it.

So I was glad, just now, to have a friend tell me I shouldn't have used chlorine bleach. Where was I when everybody else was learning there's more than one kind of bleach?

It temporarily threw me, that yellow stain, but I'm myself again, cheerful, desperately, making allowances. Wrong bleach. Not my fault.

No sooner had that mystery been cleared but, in a moment of inattention for which I will just have to forgive myself, I tossed Bill's pink Polo shirt in with the dark wash.

I did remember not to throw it in the dryer. Instead I hung it up wet in the bathroom, where it looks very nice, except for the smallish black streaks along the sides and the brown one on the top, from the rusty hanger.

It's Time to Think Like a Landlord

One day a linoleum tile came loose in our kitchen floor, near the refrigerator. It wasn't the end of the world, but it left a black hole, and the particle board between the tiles and the wood had soaked up refrigerator water.

We instinctively did what we have always done when household repairs are necessary: ignored it for months, then stretched out a hand to call the landlord. "If you think we're going to put up with this at the rent we pay, you're crazy!"

Then we remembered we signed a lot of papers and spent a lot of money so we wouldn't have a landlord anymore, and now we don't.

Once we remembered *we* were the landlords, we decided the problem had been greatly exaggerated. A simple throw rug was the answer. True, the refrigerator door would run into the rug every time it was opened, but it could easily be straightened out again each time.

Unlike most landlords, though, we lived there. Straightening the rug began to wear on our nerves, and we realized we had to get a new floor.

How much could it cost, really?

"Oh, you're looking at around $1,500," said the man at the floor store. "It's a big kitchen."

Fifteen hundred *dollars?* That was a trip to Club Med!

Then we caught ourselves: That was Tenant Thinking. We had to switch to Owner Thinking. Owners look at your Mexico tan and wonder how many new floors that set you back.

We weren't about to pay that. That was for dupes. It might be our first floor job, but we could look around, find a deal.

My ex-brother-in-law in the ceramic tile business came over, measured, and said he could do it in three nights at the special price of $1,500, including the tiles.

That's when I remembered that not only are ceramic tiles cold, but also ex-brothers-in-law aren't worrying about having to face you across the table at Thanksgiving anymore. They're thinking of you as what you are: a tile customer.

Over a glass of wine, Steve, a contractor friend, said of course we'd also want to replace the fraying particle board under the tiles with state-of-the-art structure board. It would cost six or seven hundred more, he added, but we would have the satisfaction of doing the job right.

Then a man named Ken said he'd put new sheet linoleum down in one day for $1,600. When we said no, he offered to come down $100 on the price.

This only confirmed our suspicion that he had built a trip to Carmel into the original bid, but we said sure. We were hoping that he needed the job really bad, and that we could cunningly take advantage of this. Also, he seemed to have no problem with the present particle board.

We were so pleased we hardly noticed that after months of researching better deals, we were back at $1,500. Besides, by now we disliked the floor so much that ripping it up seemed a reasonable alternative to mopping it.

We hired Ken, who moved out the appliances and put in white linoleum with little black diamonds. Morgan came home and said thanks for remembering that she had wanted a refrigerator in her room, but could she get something a little smaller?

I'll be glad when we get the floor paid off, because it turns out rainwater leaks into the closed bathroom window. After seven years of drought, who knew? I'm thinking of getting some bids to fix it.

Bill's thinking maybe a towel along the sill on wet days.

What They Don't Know
Won't Hurt Them

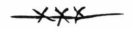

I discovered a couple of days ago that Bill, who buys and makes our morning coffee, switched to decaf months ago. He had the grace to look sheepish when I stormed into the bedroom and confronted him.

"I didn't think you'd notice," he said.

The night before, I hadn't had time to make a cup of instant coffee before an evening meeting, so I went to get a coffee bean to chew on. To my surprise, all three of our white bags of coffee beans were marked decaf: Swiss decaf, Colombian decaf, hazelnut creme decaf. No wonder I was feeling sleepy.

"When were you planning to tell me?" I said.

"Well, never," he said. He said he had reduced the amount of caffeine we were drinking gradually, over months, before cutting it out completely. "You never make the coffee, so how would you know? I had no idea you ate coffee beans. I was afraid if I did tell you, you'd want the caffeine back. And I've been feeling so much better since I stopped drinking caffeine."

"I see."

"You're not mad, are you?"

Mad? Me? Of course not. I'm just glad to have an explanation for those puzzling new health problems I've been having—pounding headaches and a tendency to lapse into unconsciousness before noon. This won't affect our relationship at all. I don't even mind remembering last week, when I couldn't get to sleep until 3 a.m. and had to teach an early Saturday class—and Bill very nicely got up with me so he could send me off with a cup of hot coffee.

Anyway, I understand. As couples march in lockstep toward the boneyard, differences are bound to arise. You can't agree on everything, and maybe one of you wants to give up coffee, and the other hasn't thought about it but might not be ready to. The two of you drink out of the same pot. What's the one who wants to give it up supposed to do?

In the book *Heartburn*, the philandering husband hates onions, but Nora Ephron puts them in his food anyway because how can you cook without them? I used to slip polyester-blend shirts in my ex-husband's wardrobe, and despite his contention that he could wear only all-cotton, I didn't see him tearing off his shirt in the middle of his English class, swearing that he couldn't breathe.

Deceit is widespread in modern relationships. My friend Donna, exasperated when her husband, Michael, kept absentmindedly walking off with the pen she keeps next to the note pad in the kitchen, now hides the pen in the silverware drawer. My friend Dirk tells his lover, Ray, that they have to be everywhere a half-hour before they do.

This is marital lying, a special category of lie. It's not a white lie, meant to spare your feelings. It's a pink lie. It means what you don't know, angel-face, won't hurt you.

Oh, I want to be fair. Of course Bill didn't actually lie. I never said, "Morning, sweetie. Coffee have caffeine in it today?" Michael, futilely searching the kitchen for the pen that used to be right by the phone, never said, "You wouldn't be by any chance hiding that pen in the silverware drawer, would you, lamb chop?"

But with each cup of coffee he brought to my desk, Bill lied. Each time Michael looked in vain for something to scribble with, Donna's nose grew.

Marital lies are hard to resist. He *says* he's allergic to garlic, but doesn't he really mean he's squeamish about the smell or that he associates garlic with turtlenecks and a three-day beard? Why not slip it in anyway, since the food will taste so much better?

In fact, I have to admit myself that sometimes after doing the wash, I find one of Bill's socks still behind the hamper. I want to keep the pair together, but I don't want to wash the clean one all over again. So I have to make a decision.

In fact today might have been one of those days, Bill, when circumstances forced me to let you go to work wearing one dirty sock and one clean one.

I'm really sorry. I didn't think you'd notice.

Courting the Perfect Couple

We were at our table in the Chinese restaurant, waiting for another couple: He's the minister of an Episcopal church, and she teaches English in a Catholic high school. It was our first date with them, and we were eager to make a good impression.

When Bill and I got married, we thought the horrors of dating were behind us forever. We would walk through life hand in hand, looking into each other's eyes.

Now we've discovered that we're dating as much as ever, searching as before for the perfect one, the one who will laugh at our jokes and tell us all their secrets and stick with us through thick and thin. The only difference is that we're now looking for the perfect *couple.*

With some couples we were mad about her but hated him, or the other way round. To solve this, we kept trying to introduce our single friends to each other, trying to make them into couples for us to date. It worked spectacularly in one case, except they fell head over heels in love and neither of them had time for us anymore. In another it backfired: We found we had made two people we both liked into a couple that neither of us liked much. Her excess energy made him look lackluster; his dry wit made her seem fatuous. We had them over for dinner and heartily wished one of them would go home.

Or they had a baby. Couples with babies, like couples with newly remodeled kitchens that they did all the work on themselves, are best off with each other. I was part of a couple like that: Our way of entertaining adult company during those years was to urge Morgan into the middle of the room to do her dance.

While you are not actually going to sleep with the other couple, there should be some sexual attraction, some undercurrent, some flirting. If a woman looks at Bill with obvious admiration, I may make a mental note to scratch her eyes out later, but it reminds me how nice-looking he is, which I am likely to forget if I'm home squabbling with him about where to put the couch. But we also want the couple we're dating to be in love with each other. We want to warm ourselves at their fire.

They should also be prone to blurting things out. Good couples are like good movies: You enjoy them at the time, but what you really like is discussing them afterward. Gossip about other people is one of the world's underrated pleasures. Couples make the best gossip because you see them together and can thus store up tidbits—dropped hints, funny looks, odd remarks—for the ride home.

We know one couple who just drive us nuts. They're always breaking up—he storms off to New York to produce a show, he comes back, they show up together, and they tell us *nothing*.

Sometimes we find the perfect couple, but they live too far, or they're going to India, or they're breaking up, or they are impervious to our charms. We have had our hearts stomped on by couples who led us on, even camping with us, then never called. Was it something we said? Something we did? One couple pops up here and there at parties, smiles, leads us into dazzling conversation, then disappears again, leaving us wondering if it might have worked out, if only we had got their number.

Our new couple arrives at the restaurant, and a lot of animated conversation follows. A week later, we got a note from him. It said his wife had told him he talked too much at the dinner. They had argued about this, and he had written to apologize, "if I really did talk too much." I wrote back, saying don't be silly, we were the ones who babbled like teenagers.

We're hoping they'll call us.

How Cody Was Added to the Family

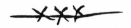

For a long while before we drifted over to the dog show last Sunday, Bill and I had talked about a dog.

I think it started when we got back from camping up on the Mendocino coast with my twin sister and her husband and their dog, Sunny. Another dog there, a huge rottweiler puppy named Taz, had been tied to a tree while his owner went abalone diving.

It reminded me of a time when I was traveling in Switzerland by myself. I had thought I was happy to be so profoundly on my own, having a grand experience, when I was caught by the sight of a small yellow dog waiting for his master outside a department store in Geneva. The dog kept peering in through the glass, his whole body anticipating the moment when his master would come back into view. I watched, and found myself wishing desperately, hopelessly, that the dog was waiting for me. It was my first clue that I was lonely.

It's been a long time since either Bill or I had a dog. When we went for a walk at that campground, we took the huge puppy, who had reportedly been through obedience school but hadn't, I think it's fair to say, retained much. We took him because he just wanted it so much. You could see it all over his face.

When we started talking about getting a dog of our own, we pretended it was for Patrick. A boy needs a dog, we said to each other. But Patrick was out playing basketball, his real passion, when we started reading ads and going to the pound.

Bill wanted to adopt the first one we saw there, a two-year-old, soft-eyed creature who reminded him of Cody, the dog he'd had as a kid. He also wanted the one two cages down, and the brown dog next to that, though it looked around fifty years old and its card admitted it wasn't housebroken. Could we just take it for a walk? he asked.

I had to haul Bill out of there. I was particular. I wanted a high-spirited dog that would nonetheless fall into a deep sleep whenever it saw me go near the keyboard.

When he wasn't falling for the sweet mutts at the pound, Bill was particular too. He wanted a barkless, odorless, nonshedding sort of bow-wow, a sort of un-dog. There is such a dog, a basenji, but the ads say "loves to run," meaning it will eat your apartment for breakfast.

For a long time, we hesitated. A dog would make demands. Its nails would click on the floor. It would whine and wake us up and pee on the rug and eat our shoes. We couldn't go away on weekends if we had a dog. We never *have* impulsively gone away for the weekend, but now we wouldn't be able to decide to.

We drove out to the dog show in the pouring rain and walked around all day, strolling by everything from Chihuahuas to Irish wolfhounds. We were just looking. Then we came to the Shetland sheepdogs, or shelties, and saw Cody, a seven-month-old who had just finished first in his puppy class but had nonetheless washed out of show biz. His breeder had decided he was too lively and unserious ever to be a champion.

We bought him. We named him fast, before we got him home and the kids insisted on calling him Snowball or Lassie—or El Norte or Emmett or Monterosa, Morgan's actual suggestions.

Now we have a dog to worry about, in addition to the boy and the girl and the bird I don't think I've mentioned, a canary named Jack who sings as if his life depended on it, and the cat who watches the bird in its cage as if it were a special kind of cat television.

We have more ties than ever. In a way, I think this is the idea. Or it's just as my dad says, that it is dangerous to go for extended periods with nothing to wag its tail at the sound of your voice.

Being
A
Grown-up

My First Shrink

At 5 p.m. on a Wednesday night in my thirty-seventh spring, I find myself barreling through the city in the dusk, heading for my appointment with the shrink. My first ever.

I did some shopping for this guy, asking candidates how threatened they felt about being interviewed for the position of my analyst. One growled, "What's your problem?" What's yours, buddy?

I arrive at the block of California Street where all the shrinks huddle together. I am obviously repressing some parking spaces and denying others, because it takes a while. While I circle, I decide I resent Dr. Bruce Levin for wanting $90 an hour to talk to me when I am prepared to be fascinating.

Also, I wonder if he will appreciate finding out that I am not preshrunk. I come not from the self-indulgent, self-absorbed, shrink-visiting anal-retentive middle classes, but from the people—the oral-explosive, drinking-class Irish. We don't even know shrinks. They live in another neighborhood.

In short, I am offering Levin a wild and untended orchard. Nobody has been here before him, squinting nearsightedly at my psyche, spraying what needs pruning. He can just stroll around and pick up the fallen apples.

I have, on the drive over, tried to rehearse my little speech. What brings me to your office, doctor? "There's this guy who doesn't want me to change but wishes I were different . . ." Great. To get a guy? That's a real grown-up reason to hie me to a shrinkery. Nah. "I'm trying to write a book about my family . . . " Nope. True, but too detached.

What brings me here? I guess it's time to kick over a few rocks, see what's under there. God, what an awful image. Must remember to tell the shrink.

Here's the door. I'm right on time, 5:50. If you're early, you're anxious; if you're late, you're hostile; if you're on time, you're compulsive. Pick up that apple.

Sounds of snuffling come from a nearby door—someone is getting her $90 worth. Since I have a few minutes to spare, I fill out the medical form. "When did the illness begin?" it says. That stumps me. I pause, then write down "January 3, 1952"—my birthdate. It occurs to me that this is what the insurance companies would call a pre-existing condition, so I crumple it up.

Oh, here comes Levin, tall, skinny, halo of curly hair, around my age. Oh, great. My type. Let the transference begin.

We pad down a hallway past soothing watercolors and into a spacious office; then we take armchairs on opposite sides of the room. Discomfort rises in my breast. He's too far away, and the fat blue box of Kleenex is too near. It's the only thing on my side of the room, like a challenge. Use me. Cry. Be good at this.

I begin by prattling, hear my own voice in my ears, telling him about my boyfriend, about my family, about what has set me, ever so tentatively, on the path to self-exploration.

Levin smiles and speaks with the familiarity of an old friend. This is hopeless. He's snowed even though I have asked him to flag me—raise his hand or something—when I am being glib or evasive. I need a female shrink.

After twenty minutes, he digs out his appointment book and I dig out mine and we discuss the time of the next appointment. I wonder why he feels it necessary to do this on my time. His childhood is beginning to interest me.

He remarks that at this point in their lives, most people are pretty happy with their characters. I might conclude in a few weeks that I'm OK. This worries me. But I guess you bring a shrink a vague problem, you get a vague solution. Garbage in, garbage out.

By this time, I have got off myself completely and am rattling on about my boyfriend, and the shrink doesn't even notice. So much for raising his hand . . . . Oops, hour's up. At exactly 6:50, my new friend Bruce abruptly loses interest in my monologue, though I think I am having interesting insights into my boyfriend's character.

Leaving, I notice Bruce has two heavy wooden doors, one right after the other. This guy needs a shrink. "I noticed you have two doors," I say brightly. "Did I pass the test?" I picked up on my own need to pass tests— did Bruce? Did he notice my earlier reference to wanting to do well? Is he there? Hello? Do I like have an attitude problem, and if not, where can I find one, cheap, before next Wednesday?

The Benefits of Being Fired

I've been talking to a friend of mine who needs to be fired. Someone must march into her office, sweep her Rolodex, memos, file folders and her gummy old coffee cup into a cardboard box, demand her keys, throw her coat over her shoulders, and kick her out into the sunshine.

It's not that she hates her job. She doesn't. It's just that when she walks into her office after a long weekend, the walls entomb her. She's bored. It's a good job, but she's done it too long.

Boredom may seem a colorless little problem, when heaped next to the world's great angsts, but boredom, I read recently on a bathroom wall, is "rage stretched thin." For my money, it has the feel of the grave.

She could quit, my friend could, but that's rough. Leaving a job, particularly a secure, well-paying one, is like leaving a lover or a parking space.

How can she be sure she'll find another one? What about the car payments, the rent, the neat little title on her business cards, so handy for explaining who she is?

Of all the people I know who feel stifled by their jobs, only a handful have left without another gig waiting. This takes pluck—not to mention some savings—and the luxury of having no one dependent on you.

One of them is my friend Diane. Until last January, she lived on the Peninsula and worked as a staff writer for a house and garden magazine. It was the perfect job—a generous salary, pleasant colleagues, the scent of roses wafting across her desk from the garden out the window.

Every day she put on a skirt or a tasteful pantsuit, per the dress code, and sat at her tidy cubicle to write about floor tiles, low-cost fenestration and the best season for pruning roses.

At ten in the morning a little bell rang, summoning her and her colleagues to the pastry and coffee wagon. When the bell rang again, she returned to her desk. At thirty-nine, the prime of her life, Diane found she was looking forward to retirement and her comfortable pension.

Once an article of hers was nearly in print when an alert copy editor said, "Didn't you write this before?" Diane was appalled to see that she had sleep-written the same story about kohlrabi, with an almost identical lead, that she had penned a year before.

When her tenth anniversary arrived, Diane's colleagues paraded around a large conference room unfurling their wonderful surprise—every article she had ever written stitched together like a banner. As she stood there, eating crumbling anniversary cake and watching ten years of her life go by in a blur of redwood decks, blue jays and rock gardens, a country song lyric began to play in Diane's mind: "Take this job and shove it. I ain't working here no more."

Diane shoved that job, though her colleagues gathered around, worried at such rashness, and prophesied, "You'll be back."

She didn't go back. She took what the Germans call a *wanderjahr*, a year to wander. For the first six months she was still "going like a freight train," signing up for classes, attending seminars, interviewing people in fields that interested her. Then she just sat still for a while admiring the flowers that grew in her back yard.

Now Diane lives in the city. She has a new job that pays far less and interests her far more.

Meanwhile, we left my other friend ejected from her office and dumped on the grass, while the breeze blows her files down to Mexico. I think we should just leave her there, drinking in the sunshine, until she realizes she's still alive, still kicking. And she's free. She has it back, her god-given, one and only, once-in-a-lifetime life.

Go Ahead and Scold, I'm Used to It

It was in the paper: Some joggers drove to Ross, a wealthy town in Marin County, chatted loudly and played the radio while preparing for their early-morning run, and came back to find a deep scratch running the length of their car. A note warned the joggers to be more considerate next time.

This is a good example of the two kinds of people there seem to be in the world: the scolders and the scoldees.

I'm a natural-born scoldee, the kind of person who will reach for any drink that happens to be near her or absentmindedly cut you off in traffic and then wonder what you're honking about. A scoldee will drive blithely into the parking space you're waiting for and never even see you. If scoldees spot the sandwich you made for yourself for lunch in the fridge, they'd just eat it, and never ask themselves how it got there. Scoldees sail right up to the cashier without noticing there's a line.

As a scoldee, I'm always bumping up against the other kind, the scolder. Scolders never drink other people's drinks or park in people's driveways, and they don't want you to, either.

Scolders seem to spot me even when I'm not doing anything wrong at the moment. I was sitting on the curb on 18th Street, waiting for Bill to come out of the cactus store, when a woman and a man came by.

"Is that yours?" the woman said sharply. A Twinkies package fluttered on the pavement at my feet. "No," I said. "Well, do you want to grab it and put it in the trash?" the woman answered.

I don't litter, but I'm a scoldee, and I look as if I might.

Scolders are always watching scoldees. I once bent down to pick a flower on a deserted block early Sunday morning, and a scolder burst out of her house like a rifle shot, screen door banging, to bellow, "Put that flower down!"

Somehow the two kinds always seem to get most on each other's nerves when it comes to cars, and to extensions of cars, such as driveways and streets and neighborhoods.

A scoldee I know returned to her car one hot afternoon to find an enraged woman standing by it. "How long have you been gone? Your dog might have died in there!" The driver of the car felt terrible (the shade had moved), but her apologies did nothing to deflect the other's rage.

It was as if all the sorrows of her world, every wrong ever done her, had been poured into this moment, as if she were that overheated spaniel, and finally the second woman actually hit the side of the car with the flat of her hand.

A few years ago, when I wasn't used to street parking, I'd circle the block endlessly, looking for a place big enough for my car. Sometimes I would look up to see curtains twitching, as the garage owners (natural-born scolders) watched me from their living rooms.

One morning I found someone had crumpled one of my windshield wipers as a warning not to block his driveway again. I had left him room to get out: I thought that was the idea, for him to get out. That's how a scoldee thinks. That's why we give scolders nervous breakdowns.

Scoldees are different. We don't care if you sit on our car, and we sit on yours without dreaming that you'd mind. You can park in our driveway if you leave a note to say where you are.

But the scolder is easily annoyed when his own rights are violated, and when he retaliates, he retaliates against property. He crumples a windshield wiper or scratches a car. You are hurting him by hurting his property, and he thinks this is the way he should hurt you. It never occurs to him that he might let the air out of the tires of that car owned by noisy joggers, to trade inconvenience for inconvenience.

The Dubious Pleasures of
a Good Long Sulk

We had agreed I would follow Bill to the tire store across town, as I had no idea where it was. This plan worked fine until the first stoplight, when he sped through the yellow and I got caught on the red and watched him disappearing around a corner.

I spent the next 45 minutes driving all over town, going to two wrong addresses, trying to find the tire store.

As I drove, seething, my knuckles whiter and whiter on the steering wheel, I wondered how many days were going to pass before I'd be able to speak to Bill in a really warm tone of voice again. I was cursing the day I was born and the day I met Bill, but I was also, underneath, enjoying the feeling of being flat-out mad.

Then the bottom fell out of my fine black mood. I found the tire store and stalked into the waiting room where Bill was lounging with a magazine.

He put his arms around me. "I'm so sorry," he said. "It's all my fault. Since you're the one who recommended this tire store in the first place, I was sure you knew the way."

As he spoke, any hope of making him suffer as I had suffered flickered out. I didn't get to be mad for days. I didn't even get to be mad for as long as I'd been searching for the tire store. We just went off food shopping, as planned, while they put new front tires on my car.

This is the disadvantage of a mature relationship. You miss the satisfactions of a really Richard Nixonian sulk, of getting mad and staying mad, and not listening to any efforts to bring you out of it.

When you sulk, you're never in the wrong. You're the Queen of the May, the gloriously innocent party hugging your injustices to your breast. Access to your person is restricted. Windows are slammed down, doors boarded over. You can pretend you adore the abalone shell earrings, then seethe secretly every time you remember you got *him* a jacket and an expensive jogging suit.

When the person you are punishing is absent, sulking is transformed into that other delicious but necessarily more solitary activity, brooding. I've spent many a happy hour vacuuming topsoil off the venetian blinds after a fight with someone, letting the phone ring while luxuriously remembering my injuries and rehearsing my remarks.

I used to be so good at feeling wronged that I didn't always require a partner. As I pushed my cart through the aisles at the grocery store, I'd get mad at my roommate for telling me not to buy diet drinks when it was none of his business.

It made no difference to me that he was out of town when we had this falling out.

Sulking and brooding, and that other lost pleasure of immaturity, martyrdom, make the other person miserable and allow him to appreciate the unhappiness he has caused you. This satisfies your child's sense that if people upset you, they have to pay. It magically returns you to that happy childlike stage when you were the center of the universe and the tedium of considering other people's feelings was still far in the future.

Mature fights are by contrast dreary and unsatisfying. You have to make concessions, admit you may have been wrong or cop to what's really bothering you—for instance, that he held all the money in the garage sale when you wanted to hold some of it.

Or, worse, you have to just forget it, never even tell her you noticed the huge chip she gouged in the doorway when she was trying the bookshelf out in various new locations.

All mature fights do, really, is clear the air and promote lasting relationships. And you're just not always in the mood for that, are you?

The Taxing Times We Live In

I was whining about this year's tax bill to my friend Sally. She has been through a lot with the feds, thanks to a successful small business she forgot to mention on her form one year. "It's been trial and error," she says, "but I've learned that it pays to be sensitive to the needs of the IRS."

It's because I'm sensitive to the needs of the IRS that I took a class in money management. I was also tired of my mother calling up to urge me to invest my nonexistent money in tax-exempt funds. (Although I may have brought that on myself. I told her my idea of money management is to tear little holes in the bottom of a check so it takes a couple of extra days to clear.)

Seven or eight of us were sitting around a linen-covered table, miserably contemplating our fiscal sins.

"How are you going to get to the point where your money is working for you, instead of you working for it?" Lois, the instructor, asked us.

I had no idea. My money doesn't stay around long enough to look for work. When I tried to save, I only ended up agreeing with Ernest Haskins, who said, "Save a little money each month, and at the end of the year you'll be surprised at how little you have."

I was sitting with my arms folded and my feet planted on another chair, listening balefully to lectures on the importance of balancing our checkbooks, CDs, IRAs, Sep-IRAs (an IRA by marriage, I think), and somebody called Fannie Mae.

I wanted Lois to get through to me, to say something to make me feel less bored and overwhelmed by the prospect of money management. I'm going to be one of the 76 million geezers fighting over Social Security scraps one of these days. But I'm still depressed about the taxes I owe to the IRS, an organization cold and merciless in its efficiency.

I did perk up once, when a guy at the back said, "You know, I find that running a magnet across the little numbers at the bottom of the check works even better than tearing."

Lois, wincing at this, went on chalking discouraging statistics on the board. I was surreptitiously getting into my coat, preparing to slip away, when she said, "Forty percent of Americans overpay their taxes simply out of their quaking fear of the IRS. They plant that fear. Watch for a big story right before April 15—some clown being hauled off to the slammer for income tax fraud."

I took my coat off. They plant that fear?

According to a survey in this month's *Money* magazine, nearly *half* the 36 million letters mailed to taxpayers last year contained grievous blunders, most of them clerking errors. We sent in a estimated $7 billion we didn't owe.

This got my interest. Turns out I'm not up against an infallible bureaucracy, but some poorly trained, underpaid clerk sitting in an airless office somewhere, busily typing any old thing into an antiquated IRS computer. Like the rest of us, he's resentful as hell, and he sure isn't in the mood to be sensitive to my need to hang onto my $841.

It's a scene right out of *Catch-22*, with Yossarian still bucking for a Section 8—*only now he's typing the letters the IRS sends you.*

This news is certainly going to make me pay more attention. I haven't got one of those crank communications from the IRS yet, but I'm going to double-check my own figures before I fork over a month's rent.

Could it be time to revive that old "Question Authority?" bumper sticker?

At the very least, we could try scribbling "You must be kidding!" across the next letter the IRS sends and mail it back.

Adulthood Isn't All It's Cracked Up to Be

It was Sunday, and my family was out back of my sister Robin's house, drinking beer and singing along as my brother Shannon played his guitar. I was crooning along in my tuneless way, "There Is a House in New Orleans"—afraid that everybody would stop suddenly and hear.

It's an old fear. When I was little, and sang along to the radio in the back seat, this same brother made fun of me, but I wasn't worried. I thought as soon as I figured out what he knew about singing that I didn't, I would be able to sing like Shannon.

I never fully shook off my childhood faith that life would, as I grew up, deliver to me all its secrets. Though I was a grubby kid playing in dirt, I saw myself as a grown-up woman wearing a black dress, moving gracefully through crowded rooms filled with chandeliers and polished glass. In this fantasy, the music was classical, the food exquisite and my clothes exceedingly stylish.

I was patient. I learned to tie my shoes, to ride a bike, to type, to drive, to hold down a job. But I never learned to like the sorts of things I myself equated with being an adult, with being smart.

And now I am 39. Yesterday someone called and asked me what my favorite song was, and I put down the hotdog I was eating, wiped a drop of mustard from my periwinkle fleece warm-up suit from Mervyn's and admitted it was the great rock 'n' roll standard, "Shout."

Everybody I know has gone by me. My sister Adrian, who once strapped on cowboy guns with me and sang "He's So Fine," was blasting Pavarotti in her house in Ukiah the last time I was up, the turncoat. Bill listens to KKHI; Sylvia dresses in the latest style while listening to jazz.

I've tried to hide it. Guiltily, I would switch the radio from "Billy Don't Be a Hero" to a classical station when I got out of my car. I hid my diet orange drink behind the San Pellegrino water, and declared my $15 glass of wine to be wonderful when I actually preferred the gallon-jug variety that goes straight to the calves.

I pretended to be out of coffee beans when I was drinking instant coffee until one day Bill caught me. He said with horror, "It isn't that it's easier. You actually *prefer* it." I'm the one they mean in the British commercial that says, "Take a glass of fine crystal, or, for you Americans, anything that doesn't leak."

In *When Harry Met Sally . . .* one character, trying to wrestle a wagon wheel coffee table out of her living room, tells her boyfriend that most people think they have a good sense of humor and good taste, but it can't be true for all of them.

She's right, of course. Not everyone has what it takes to appreciate a fine wagon wheel coffee table when he sees one.

I have tastes. It's just that some of them seem to have been arrested around age twelve, by some unspeakable trauma. I spent the summer of that year sitting in a chair on the front porch, reading *Reader's Digest Condensed Books* and waiting for a cute paperboy to pass by.

My tastes in furniture, books and men have evolved since then, but whatever music was playing, whatever I was eating, whatever I was wearing set my preferences for life.

I've stopped waiting. And it has stopped mattering. I no longer lunge to change the radio station. I'm more likely these days to roll the window down and jack the music up.

Meanwhile, on Robin's porch, we're on to "Where Have All the Flowers Gone?" I belt out "Long time pas-sing" and Shannon looks over, raising an eyebrow. His look confirms it: Life delivers some secrets and withholds others. I sing out anyway, my voice wilting flowers on a distant hill. Nobody ever said I couldn't sing at all.

Just Scoot a Little Bit Closer

I had my annual gyn appointment this morning with the affable Dr. Jones at Kaiser. I have, to my horror, become used to this experience. I could read a book during the exam and actually remember what I read.

It wasn't always this way. I remember my first exam, when I was 17. I had been staring unseeingly at magazines for some time when a voice said, "The doctor will see you now."

They didn't have to rub it in, I thought.

I was led to a tiny room, handed a piece of tissue paper, told to put it on.

Left alone, I was confused. Did I take everything off the top, too? What if I did and the doctor looked at me as if to say, "Whoa, we got *carried away,* didn't we?" Did I leave my socks on? And what was I supposed to do with my clothes, just sling them over the chair as if I were getting ready for bed?

A long time had passed since the nurse left. For all I knew, the doctors had got out of their lease and moved away, forgetting the shivering patient in the second room on the left.

I stuck my underwear in the pockets of my jeans, rolled everything else into a ball, and then experimented with various ways of wearing the piece of tissue paper I had been given. Leave it open in the front for the breast exam, or open in the back, letting him tear open as needed? Were those armholes, or were they to make the breast exam easier? Forced to decide, I sort of stuck it on in front, then hopped up to the table.

The doctor, when he showed up, started chatting with me about everything under the sun, movies he had seen, the weather, everything. As he began the exam, he seemed not to notice what he was doing at all, except he would say very casually, "Just scoot down a bit."

I moved down the table a half inch or so. It was not the direction I wanted to go in.

"Just a bit more." He squinted, looked and gestured again, like a man guiding a truck backing up to the dock. "Whoa, that's good."

"Now try to relax," he said, taking what looked like dental instruments out of, from the feel of them, a nearby refrigerator. "This will pinch a little," he said. I answered, desperately, that I loved *Midnight Cowboy*, what did he think of it?

"That's it," the doctor said after a while, smiling. "Nothing to it. See you next year."

Nothing to it. I'd get the results of my Pap smear in the mail.

He left so I could get dressed. They are allowed to see parts of you that you yourself hadn't got around to having a good look at, but it would be a huge breach of ethics, not to mention embarrassing all around, for them to watch you get dressed.

I got my clothes on and walked into the sunlight. I had had my first gyn checkup. I was a woman.

Now, dozens of such appointments and two kids later, my exams are a piece of cake. Dr. Jones, a real chatterbox, said today that he could find nothing wrong with me, then started to talk cheerfully about how many people my age are dropping dead of colon cancer. "But now we have this great test," he added.

I hoped it would be something men had to come in for this time. Tissue-paper gowns and icy instruments in unfamiliar places (while patient and doctor chat determinedly about those Niners) might tell them what we'd been subjected to all our adult lives.

But no. You mail your sample in.

They couldn't do that for Pap smears, I suppose.

Persecuted by Warm People

I'm always sad to see the end of Indian summers, that blast of warmth between our cool summers and winters, partially because I'm the kind of person who's always cold. I think it's because I'm a twin, doomed to shiver through life, missing my sister's warmth in the womb.

This is not a problem. I sleep with a small extra blanket that covers my side of the bed, wear a light woolen vest under my T-shirts, buy so many jackets that they hang from pegs all over the house, a kind of interior insulation.

The problem is Warm People, the ones who go around opening windows to let in a gale and kicking off blankets. Warm People don't understand. They think you're cold because you obstinately refuse to be warm. When you want to return to the car for your sweater, they can't quite keep the disbelief out of their voices. "Are you *cold?*" they ask. "But it's *not* cold." When this doesn't convince you, they go on, never losing hope of explaining this to you clearly enough so that you will get it. "You *can't* be cold."

I've been hearing this all my life, and I'm still amazed that someone can stand there and tell you you aren't cold.

Where are they getting their information?

I admit Cold People don't understand Warm People, either. Warm People don't know that happiness is not possible without heat. Nor do most of them realize their houses come equipped with a device that will heat the house at the flip of a switch. For Warm People, turning on the heat is a wild extravagance, like buying a sports car.

In 1974, I went from a series of cozily overheated, low-ceilinged apartments in balmy Marin to sharing a huge flat in a San Francisco Victorian with four roommates. The heat was never turned on. When I came down to the kitchen the first morning, one of my new roommates, Kenner, was reading the paper on a chair in the kitchen, dressed in a three-piece suit, warming his stocking feet in the open oven.

"Put on a sweater," my new roommates suggested when I showed them goosebumps the size of the Himalayas. I didn't understand this response.

For me, a *house* was a kind of sweater.

Instead of piling on clothes, which felt silly in a house, I'd wander around miserably, warming my hands on my coffee cup. I kept expecting to see a sign on the wall: "Hypothermia, the Danger Signs."

Once when everybody else had gone to the theater and I was home alone writing, I turned up the heat a little, to a comfortable 75°. It was bliss—like moving your Victorian house to a Mexican beach.

Then my roommates came home. You would think, from their reaction to being greeted at the threshold by a blast of warm air from their 4,000-square-foot Victorian, that I just tried to heat New York City instead of one little house.

Honestly.

That was many years ago. I have since acclimated, and will warm the seat of my office chair with an electric blanket and don a ski sweater before I'll heat a whole house just to warm one person working at a desk.

But Indian summer, when the city temperatures zoom upward, remains my favorite time of year. The air's soft, the sun's bright, and everywhere Warm People are sweating miserably, begging to be allowed to retreat to the shade, or to go back to the car to get rid of some layers of clothes.

"Are you too *warm?*" I say, with barely concealed astonishment. "Gee, are you sure? It isn't warm."

The Competing Lists That Define a Life

I was having such a productive day. I did some writing, went to the bank, bought orange roughie and salad for dinner, even kept my appointment for a mammogram.

When my turn came, I stood there without my blouse, reading a poster that showed pictures of women blithely putting off their mammograms. The only thing that could make me feel more smug about keeping my own appointment would be that they actually found a lump, and I was given an early cure.

The technician was brisk. I asked how many times she had done this already today and she laughed, wearily. "Fifty?"

Afterward, I went to the room where you wait for results. One by one, while I read through an entire New Yorker profile, they sent everybody else home.

"Lara? We need two more plates."

Numbly, I followed the technician back to the X-ray room. I watched to see whether she would take the same pictures again, which would mean the first ones just hadn't come out right, but she took entirely new ones. A spot on the right breast troubled her, she said, and she wanted to magnify it. "After I take these two, you can go," she said.

Extra plates. What did she think she had seen? As I drove home, I made up my mind that I would not overreact. Until the hospital called, I would forget about the second set of plates. I would just go on about my business.

By the time I hit the third red light, I was, in my imagination, back at the doctor's, getting the bad news. Six blocks later I was admiring Bill for the way he accepted a wife with one breast. By the time I turned into my driveway, my children were motherless.

That afternoon, I remembered a song called "Twenty Million Things," by a man named Lowell George. In it he sings with incredible poignancy of all the things, trivial and profound, that remained undone in his life.

As my runaway imagination transformed a mere set of extra plates into a tragic early death, I thought about my own list. What have I done, and what have I left to do?

I have lived in Paris, had two babies, published two books, been fired, worked on a movie set, owned a raccoon, been thrown out of a bar. I have read thousands of wonderful books, stretched out in the sunshine on my back steps, and been arrested. I've been to Prague, nursed a child, hitchhiked through Ireland.

What is there left? I have never cooked a turkey, never eaten escargot, never had more money than I knew what to do with. I have never been in a fight, programmed a VCR, or been to the White House. Nor have I yet bought a lottery ticket, seen a dead person, or written a novel. I have never been to Africa. I have never been to Indiana, grown old with anyone, or looked into the face of my child's child.

After dinner my friend Annie called, and I told her what I had been unable to tell Bill, which is that I was riddled with cancer. She said, "Oh, half my friends have had a second set of plates taken, it happens all the time." She congratulated me for going, said it was stupid to skip a simple test that can save your life.

A mere six weeks later, Kaiser rushed over a note saying I was fine.

If one of the things, trivial or profound, that you have never done is get a mammogram, then you should know that even my mother, of all people, finally went out and got one. She said everything was fine, and in fact she found the test kind of interesting, and she got to cross it off her list.

The Little Death in a Woman's Life

I heard Bill cursing in the bathroom. It was just a small cut, but the razor had nicked a blood vessel, and he bled profusely for an hour, leaning over the sink, swearing, throwing bloody toilet paper into the basket and dabbing at his face again and again.

I forced him to stand still while I put on a tiny Band-Aid. "That won't work! This has happened before, and I know." I put another Band-Aid on top of the first one, and the bleeding stopped.

Women are inured from their early teens to the sight of their lifeblood spilling. Each month brings a little death, the washed-out remains of a life that never began. Women leak all the time, like old refrigerators and faulty milk cartons. We know that life is messy.

I remember the exact moment when I learned that. One day in the sixth grade, all the boys were sent out of the room and we girls watched a film called *Menstruation and You*. We each received a little pink booklet that prepared us for the coming mystery of womanhood. When we were released back into the school yard, the boys looked at us in a new way, baffled, but interested.

The Period had begun its odd role in our lives, as our secret, our burden, our mystery and our excuse to get out of almost anything. By the eighth grade, the girls who had their periods lorded it over those of us who didn't, working a reference to "the curse" and cramps into every conversation, and sitting prettily on the bench doing their nails while the rest of us sweated at jumping jacks in PE.

It was no coincidence for high school girls that the school day was broken up into periods. Coach Stevens, the male teacher of my co-ed PE class my senior year, not only didn't need convincing that we were unable to dress down for volleyball, but also lived in continual fear that one of us girls might volunteer the precise nature of her indisposition. Before we could finish the sentence beginning, "Coach, I can't dress down because I got my . . ." he'd rip off a note excusing us.

He had a soul mate in the Honorable M. William Graybill of Florida, in a case written up in *Harper's* magazine. The jury was sequestered, deciding whether a man was guilty of grand theft, when Judge Graybill received a note from the bailiff saying one of the jurors had asked that "personal female products" be sent in.

Flustered, the judge ordered the jury to return to the courtroom, and said to them all (I'm quoting from the court transcript), "Have we reached a point where it is absolutely necessary that a certain juror have certain products at this particular time? If so, this court is going to declare a mistrial."

This might have been the first case of a man having a sentence ended by a period, but cooler heads prevailed (the bailiff went to the drugstore after the men put their heads together and decided it would be all right to delicately inquire about the "strength of product desired").

The article didn't mention whether the judge was married, but my guess is he wasn't. Every married man has a period to get used to, even if he's only writing "Watch Out!" in his pocket calendar.

Women are trained by the very fact of having a period to know that life doesn't always run on the rails—for example, that an unforeseen event might arrive when it isn't supposed to—for example, when you're in the jury room and completely unprepared. It happens.

The hitch comes when you whisper to the bailiff, and he delivers your message to the judge, who is, *wouldn't you know it,* one of those boys sent out to the playground while the girls were watching *Menstruation and You.*

How Do You Know You're Getting Older?

When you sit on your mother's lap anywhere, your legs embarrass you, they just go on for miles.

You notice that the other girls carry their binders against their chests, not under their arms. You start carrying yours that way, too.

Getting dressed in the bathroom, you notice that your little brother's eyes are pinned to your chest. From that moment on you dress in private.

Someone tells you that if you eat all those Oreos you'll get fat.

You do sit-ups for a long time, daydreaming that the next time you get punched in the stomach the person will be really surprised. Months go by, and no one punches you, and you realize nobody ever will again.

The lady with the candy says, "you, the big kid at the back, aren't you a little big for trick or treating?"

You stop wanting to be a boy and start wanting to go with one.

You stand up way across the room when you watch cartoons on TV, so it'll be clear to whoever comes in that you're not really watching.

Your mom tells you you're too big to jump on the couch like that, you'll break it.

You look at the calves of your legs and they're really fat all of a sudden.

A boy grabs your hand and tells you to either clean 'em or cut 'em.

You call your mother from Reno just to give her a scare.

You walk home, mad as hell, three miles from the bar at 2 a.m. after telling your ex-husband that of course he can go out with your sister. You don't mind a bit.

You walk into a hardware store and the woman smiles and asks you when the baby is due. You tell her you had it yesterday.

You turn thirty, and think, "My God, this is my life." You had thought this was your pre-life, the audience warm-up, the corridor leading to the room where your life was.

You start putting cream on your face every night and morning.

People in stores start calling you ma'am.

You get big freckles on your legs that will never go away.

You wish your friends would stop looking so much like grown-ups.

Your dentist stops talking about cavities and starts in on gum disease.

At 11:30, everybody leaves your party so suddenly you suspect another one must be re-forming on the sidewalk, but no, they're all going home to bed.

You give away the Levi's 501s you have been lugging around for years, waiting for them to fit again.

You stop covertly reading miracle weight-loss stories and start covertly reading about facelifts.

It no longer surprises you that your brothers and sisters can hold down jobs.

You are just beginning to think you should be more serious about make-up when your daughter borrows waterproof mascara to go swimming.

You vote for a former police chief for mayor.

You wake up on a Thursday morning in January and discover that your once youthful twin sister, a person you shared a crib with, the person who showed up promptly for all your birthday parties and elbowed you out of the way in every family picture, is turning forty the next day.

Being
A
Writer

The Joy of Being Your Own Boss

You would think that a person working alone in a house almost every day, as I do, would be free from what you put up with in offices: demanding bosses, shirking employees and office politics.

You would think.

I have worked at home, most of the time, for three-and-a-half years, and it turns out that instead of escaping any of this, I have simply made the process more efficient by combining the demanding boss and the shirking employee *in the same body.*

Monday morning, my house. The first to arrive at the office is the shirking employee, wearing two robes and doggy slippers. She did no house-work at all over the weekend, but now that it's time to start writing, she notices the computer needs dusting, and, look at that, so does the radio and the floor.

When she sprints off to get the vacuum, though, the boss makes one of her strange cameo appearances, like Bette Davis popping up in a Mel Gibson movie. "What do you think you're doing?" she says.

The boss won't let her touch the unfolded laundry, which, ignored all weekend, now emits a siren call from the living room couch. Or let her train the cat to use the scratching post, or repot the fern that fell off the fence in last weekend's storm. If only I could repot the fern, the employee thinks, then I would be happy.

Instead the shirking employee slinks back to the computer. "Can I just run out and get the dry-cleaning?" she whispers.

The boss relents. "Go ahead," she says. Her smile turns evil. "I'll just leave this work on your desk, where you can get to it when you can. I promise, no one else will touch it."

The employee is free to do what she likes, but it's the freedom of the emancipated daughter who discovers, to her horror, that her mother has somehow crept inside her and is making her wipe up the water drops in the sink.

As the morning wears on, the employee begins to wonder if there is anybody else left on earth. She burns a $3 Duraflame log in the fireplace to make it cozy.

"I work hard," she mutters, though no one has said anything. Her only office mate is a dog who watches the street from the couch.

The cat who used to have this job has let her know this is just about the last straw. But the cat had taken a lot of catnaps on the job, and many of them right on the employee. The cat will have to work his way back up from the bedroom.

When the phone rings, the boss snatches it up. "Come directly to the point," she snaps.

It's a friend calling with gossip. "For you," the boss says, handing the phone to the shirking employee. Her look says, "*What* did we decide about personal calls?"

But the mail is allowed. Offices have mail. When it comes, sometimes the employee opens the first envelope without checking to see whom the other ones are from. Sometimes she looks at them all first. She likes to mix it up. There isn't much excitement to look forward to after the mail has come.

Now and then the employee needs to go to the high school to have a chat with the dean, or to take the car in for a smog check, or she finds some other thinly veiled excuse not to write.

Occasionally, the boss allows this. "Fine," she says, smiling thinly. "You have the whole weekend to catch up on your work."

The shirking employee's friends all envy her, getting to go to the beach whenever she wants to. They just don't understand why she never wants to.

Going Cold Turkey on Epiphanies

There was a savage attack on epiphanies in the Sunday paper the other day. Perhaps you read it. Ian Shoales is dismayed by what he calls the Pensive Essay Syndrome. "They offer one darn epiphany after another: how Dad's den smelled after the divorce; how lost that first love seemed at the train station; how tall Pa seemed the day they laid him off."

He says family moments used to just pop up—"Hey, guess what my kid did yesterday?" Not anymore. "Today, thousands of boring moments are recollected in tranquility, painstakingly and poetically recaptured, relentlessly examined by men and women who have found, against all odds, the leisure time to write about them."

As my sister used to say, I resemble that remark (especially one crack about writers whose only contacts with the homeless are their unsuccessful relatives). I couldn't take Patrick out to the old swimming hole on his thirteenth birthday and help him throw stones at floating sticks without self-consciously treasuring the moment. I've written about getting rid of a couch that turned mean, passing the kids off as friends when trying to rent an apartment, about my dad's efforts to find himself, and my suspicion that other people were looking for him, too.

In the course of relating these experiences, I have more than once surrendered to the temptation to have a realization about human nature.

But that was the old me. I have seen the light, and I ain't gonna do that no more. My friend Annie says, "If you have a message, send a telegram."

Day one of no epiphanies. I was at home when I noticed the first leaves falling from the tree outside my bay window. My thoughts inevitably flew to another day when I was six and living in the San Geronimo Valley in a brown-shingled house with a flat dirt yard with six or seven brothers and sisters.

Leaves were falling on that day, too, I remember. The whole school was having a costume parade. We couldn't afford costumes, so Mother pinned leaves all over my dress and told me I was Autumn. At school I led the parade, but at recess I had to just stand in one place, lest I drop my leaves and turn into Winter. From that day on I realized beauty would always come at a price . . .

Jeez, sorry. Forget what I just said. I didn't realize anything as a result of that experience. It was just another bad day in the first grade. In the second grade I stole a quarter from my friend. In the fourth Dad burned down the house.

That's practically all I remember because all during my childhood I was reading. I started with Pippi Longstocking and worked my way through Terhune and Twain and kept it up right to the present moment.

Reading was a relief. I worried about everything as a child, from the leaves pinned to me to the way my dad said "crazy" when you asked him where he was going. I wondered why I was bothering to learn geometry when I was just going to die in sixty years.

None of the books presented life the way it often is—the way mine often seemed to me—superficial, fragmented, random and incoherent. Every book, every article, gave me instead human life shaped, made meaningful, sometimes made hopeful—and not necessarily in a Hallmarkian sense.

As I got older, reading about other people's lives allowed me to regard my own isolated, petty struggles with something approaching tenderness. It made me feel like part of the human race.

I felt that even reading Ian's piece. He voiced an impatience I've often felt myself, when learning that a man's life was redeemed by his friendship with his dog, or his bout with cancer was made holy by his new awareness of the kindness of strangers. In fact I think we all feel, especially as autumn approaches, a new kinship with . . .

Oh, hell.

Fax Me Some More of That Female Envy

When my friend Sinclair said, "You know, I've had a story on my mind these last years. Maybe I should try writing it down," I was very encouraging.

She knew, of course, that I was the writer of the two of us. Sinclair's an artist, a maker of prints. I was the one with the big contract with Doubleday. If I was having a little trouble writing the actual book, proceeding in tortured fits and starts and starting over every two weeks, that could be put down to my particular genius, which had to be coaxed out of hiding.

So when Sinclair faxed her first 500 words over to me—we were supposed to be writing each other 500 words a day—I was inclined to be generous, and find something to praise, no matter how small.

I hadn't sent my own 500 yet—I had junked my previous story line and was working on another one I didn't like much better—but it was understood by both of us that if I had managed to write them, I would have done a professional job.

I settled down at the desk with a cup of tea and scanned Sinclair's thin, ink-smeared sheets. After the first page, I was in shock.

She had ignored everything I have taught her about novel-writing, which is to cover six or seven years in a paragraph while making a joke, and written 500 words that made me keep turning the sheet over, looking for more. I could smell the tobacco smoke, feel the bewilderment of the little boy when his father forced him to take a drink, see the mist rising off the packed ice the ship was caught in.

Sinclair, in her ignorance, thinks that you write a book by sitting down and writing it. She has no idea you're supposed to lose heart after every third word, wondering why in God's name anyone thought you could do this, and wander out to the kitchen to rant to your beloved about your lack of talent.

It's as if a friend came along when you were changing a tire. "Here, I'll show you," the friend says, and in a trice changes the tire for you. Sinclair says, "Oh, a novel? Wait a sec, I think it goes something like this"—and types one out. "Is this the kind of thing you meant?"

I feel the stirrings of black envy, the kind that slides its fingers down your throat, because Sinclair is clearly one of those people you read about who sit down one day, shove the breakfast dishes aside, and start a novel on the back side of a PG&E bill. A year later you see them on the Larry King show, looking uncomfortable in new clothes, amazed at all the fuss.

They say you feel envy only in those areas where your identity is at stake. When I was a magazine editor and had groveled my way into a promotion, I began to get dark, stabbing looks from two women who had been my friends.

"It isn't that it happened to you," one came in to say. "It's just that it was supposed to happen to me."

"Can we still be friends?" I asked, bleakly. "No," she said, looking equally bleak. "I really don't think so."

It's a taboo subject, this one of women envying other women. We're not supposed to do it—we're supposed to be sisters, arm in arm against male tyranny, never feeling that another woman's victory takes something away from us.

Luckily for me, Sinclair still has a lot to learn. She's going strong, burying me in a blizzard of mail, but she will falter at some point, and I'll be there with helpful advice, because this is, after all, my field.

When we're done I'm going to take up printmaking. I think I'll be very good at it.

Me Is Just It, So There

A professor at a nearby college is scolding me again. He sent me a recent column of mine with the sentence, "Is it just me?" circled in red.

Says the professor, "If the sentence which I circled were declarative rather than interrogative, the subjective pronoun 'I' would be clearly indicated. Would you write, 'Me is just it'? or 'I am just it'?"

The professor is not the only one to chide me—I get letters from other readers saddened by grammatical lapses. The more things seem to be out of control generally, the more you see the grammar police out there, cruising worriedly up and down the avenue, waiting for someone to split an infinitive or pronounce "picture" as if it were "pitcher."

I even have a cookbook in which the author can't continue with her explanation of the whisk because she has remembered that some people mispronounce the word: "I am less concerned with your use of it," she concludes with exasperation, "than your pronunciation of it. Part of the current deplorable state of the language is that people don't know there is an audible difference between "weather" and "whether."

Part of the current deplorable state of the language, if you ask me, is that people spend their God-given sunlit hours to bother their heads with such tiny matters.

A few months ago, that same professor sent me a different column, this time circling the sentence, "Dad decided somebody had to light a fire under this family, and that was him."

"Your use of 'him' in today's article," he said, "is one of the common errors which, unfortunately, occur with regularity."

And that's all he saw, in a piece about my father—one I had spent weeks writing, and one in which I told the truth as well as I could. I know that errors are distracting and that they can make your reader think more about the holes in your education than about what you're saying, but I also know this stuff doesn't matter quite as much as people think it do.

OK, think it *does*. But can you find the fourteen other mistakes I've planted in this column, hotshot?

Back when I was managing editor of *San Francisco Focus* magazine, I had to pretend to care desperately about small errors, because our readers did. We could work for six months on an investigative piece proving that the Japanese had bought San Francisco and were turning it into a theme park, and get six letters. But let us spell something wrong in a classified ad, and the entire readership would go berserk, threatening to cancel their subscriptions if standards didn't improve.

If wasn't as if we weren't trying. We even kept a chart on the wall called the Department of Repetitions, Redundancies and Repetitions Department. ("Common errors that occur with regularity" would have fit right in.)

Not that I didn't wish standards would improve, myself, when I got a letter from an aspiring copy editor addressed to "Adair Lard." As my sister used to say, I resemble that remark.

Of course, it's only human to enjoy pouncing on mistakes instead of looking for what people are doing right. Who, for example, could resist pointing out that the professor who wrote to me used "which" when he should have used "that" *in every case*, and then left out the comma in the sentence, "Is this just a matter of usage or is it the way English is being taught today?"

He may be right. The problem may indeed be the way English is being taught today.

Or, who knows, it may be just I.

How I Became
So Hideously Nice
and
Other
Family
Legends

How I Became So Hideously Nice

The other day, as Patrick was poking his sister with a fork to get her out of his chair, I said automatically, "Patrick, you aren't going to amount to a hill of beans if you can't be nice."

"But I don't want to be a hill of beans," he said. "I want Morgan to get out of my chair."

He stabbed again, and Morgan, wheeling, went for his throat. As I, with studied impartiality, yelled at both kids and sent them to their rooms, I was reminded of the way sibling rivalry had ruined my own character.

I never had a room of my own, or even a womb. As a cross-eyed, mild-mannered twin competing with six manic siblings for notice, I practically had to get my hand stamped to get back into the house every time I went out in the yard.

The first born was my brother Sean, who came sliding down the chute feet first in 1948.

Mother gave Sean eleven months of her undivided attention—exactly eleven more than anyone else ever got—and then produced a sister. Connie had black curls and a nasty temper, and would just as soon pull the stuffing out of a mattress as look at it. Because of that, it was, on the whole, a relief when another sister came along in less than a year.

When Connie laid eyes on Mickey, who was big-eyed and blond and would soon be able to announce her intention to be a nurse when she grew up, she pulled out more stuffing and sometimes let her oatmeal plop from her bowl to the floor.

When Mickey was still cruising in diapers—her shapely toddler legs producing an ache in Connie's heart—Mom decided it would be nice to have a brother for Sean. She got pregnant with the ease that we have unfortunately all inherited, and Adrian and I joined the roster nine months later. Mother was written up in the *Stinson Beach News* for having five children under the age of five.

Every morning, Dad picked up his black lunch pail full of egg salad sandwiches and scuttled safely out of the house, leaving Mother to scrape the blackened oatmeal out of the bottom of the pan while patiently listening to the same knock-knock joke five times.

Then the sixth child was born. He was named Shannon, Mother and Dad having given up on more sons and only prepared girls' names this time.

Once we were all assembled (Robin, No. 7, came along nine years later), the scramble for favor began in earnest.

Sean's ploy was the most straightforward: he simply ran away around three every afternoon, crying and swearing, and came sulking back around dusk, dragging a stick through the dirt behind him and reeking of the salami he had bought on the sly.

Mother would yell at him, saying, "Running away won't solve anything, Sean," and he would nod solemnly and stand on one foot, all the time cutting his eyes at the rest of us as he basked in the glow of her anger.

Connie was too appalled to find herself in the family at all to bother. She slammed her bedroom door shut and didn't come out again until she was eighteen. Mickey was pretty—she had it easy—and Adrian, nicknamed "Chump," had the fastest legs at Lagunitas School.

Shannon could play "Red River Valley" on the piano by ear, and, if that wasn't enough, didn't hold back: When visitors came, he simply threw himself on the floor and howled and giggled until someone caught him by the feet and dragged him away.

I had none of these talents. I was tone deaf, too practical to run away, too cross-eyed to get by on looks, too timid to throw convincing tantrums.

Only one course was open to me, as I curled up in the corner of the couch, plotting, and I took unhesitatingly the role Patrick so blithely let drop: I became obsequiously, cloyingly, hideously nice.

I raked the yard into straight parallel lines, picked dripping bouquets of forget-me-nots for Mother, lent my bike to my brother when I knew he'd break it. I didn't scream to be in the front seat even when I knew perfectly well it was my turn. Mother, swatting backward to keep the other six out of the front would say, endlessly, tactlessly, "Why can't the rest of you be more like Adair?"

I'm amazed, thinking back, that the other kids didn't simply stage an accident and be rid of me. "Oh, Mom, Dare was out gathering flowers for you by the creek and slipped and fell in and hit her head and was swept out to sea; what's for dinner?"

Nevertheless, it worked. Mother beamed at me as she lifted her eyes from her novel to see me laboring earnestly over my homework (I always did it at the kitchen table, where she could see me), and that absent smile fed my conniving seven-year-old soul.

When we grew up, we all kept right on doing what we had been doing. Sean kept running away, and now lives three states away. Mickey is still pretty, and as unaware of it as she ever was.

Although she never forgave Mickey, Connie eventually came out of her room. She went through a disquieting stage as a hot-tubbing, print-buying Marin County matron and then turned into someone you can have a whale of a time with.

Adrian, a deputy sheriff, runs every morning, and lords it over all the rest of us by keeping her willowy figure while we alternately bag out and shrink with the years. Shannon, manager of a lumberyard, plays "House of the Rising Sun" at 2 a.m. on his guitar, and Robin, who came along nine years after the rest and thus escaped the warping influence of sibling rivalry, never developed any traits more unnerving than normalcy itself.

I have, as too many people will be only too glad to attest, gradually grown out of the unrelenting niceness that blighted my childhood. But it has left its mark—at least in that I require everybody to be nice to me.

That was, I suppose, always my object.

Things Were Different with This Baby

We called the baby Humphrey until she was born, which was when I was eleven. She was the seventh and the last of us kids, and she seemed like the beginning of better things for everyone. Mother declared this baby would never hear the words, "shut up." I got myself laughed at when I carefully picked her up and told her that before she knew it she'd be starting kindergarten.

Not long afterward, Mother took up with a genial Italian plumber named Joe Riboli, who brought $20 worth of Mars bars and Big Hunks in a brown bag for us whenever he arrived to take Mother out.

He called us all "kid" and called Robin "baby," but he knew her name. He was around for her entire childhood, even after he and mother stopped dating, giving her his time and his love and occasionally his money, so that the rest of us had to drop everything and follow her to the store like starved wolves to help her spend it.

One early Saturday morning when Robin was three, I lifted my head in my second-story bedroom and saw her hanging outside the window by one hand. "Robin!" I shouted, and, smiling impishly, she dropped from view. I ran in my underwear through the sleeping house to the outside porch and scooped her up, but she had dropped as lightly as a leaf, breaking only her leg.

When she grew up, she was different from the rest of us in a way that puzzled me, and even puzzled her. It wasn't just that she was taller, and blonder. She was just vivider. Feelings run through her like currents in a river, exuberance and despair and gloom and manic joy. She was scolded at a waitress job. She had been talking with her hands so much that it irritated her boss—and he was Italian.

Robin enters a room like a storm front, or a clap of thunder, and the rest of us in the family look at her, and stir restlessly on our chairs. She will plop right down on my lap, or hang a friendly elbow on my shoulder, and I will feel startled by it, and pleased.

Today Robin is married and struggling, with two small kids and a schedule that won't let her go to college despite repeated attempts. Her life comes spilling to me over the phone. She looks to her four big sisters for encouragement, making the same mistakes we made, searching our lives for clues to her own.

She needs us, but we need her, too. Often these days it's Robin I call when I'm troubled by something. I say that so and so was short with me, and I don't know why. "Call her back!" Robin exclaims. Call her back? Ask her? When I could retreat and sulk and let everything get ten times worse? "Call her right now and then call me back," she says.

That's odd advice, because that's not how we Irish manage our personal affairs. We'd rather feel hurt and resentful and stare out the window, rehearsing the wrongs the world has done us, than call anybody back. Robin broods for maybe twenty seconds, tops. Then she walks into the room and says, "Aren't you going to tell me I look nice, Mother?"

Where on earth did Robin come from? Where did she learn the things she knows?

I finally figured it out. Joe Riboli was *Italian*. She spent half her childhood hanging around his house, with his six brothers and the rest of his family. Robin is not Irish at all.

She's *Italian*.

The baby whose diaper I used to change will be twenty-nine soon. I'm glad she grew up so fast, because she has so much to teach me.

Face to Face in the Bathroom

Morgan is standing in the shower fully clothed, claiming the shower. Patrick, who had no interest in the bathroom until the second his sister went in there, swipes her outfit and hides it somewhere in the house. I wander into the bathroom to do something about all the yelling, and instead feel a sudden yearning to linger at the mirror and fiddle with my hair.

It seems to be a fact of life: A bathroom is not worth a second glance unless someone else wants it, badly. It's only then that you realize that your happiness depends on your getting into the bathroom right now and locking everybody else out.

I discovered this early, back in our family home in Lagunitas. We had one tiny bathroom at the end of the house, and seven fanatically modest Irish children, each one of whom would go to pieces if someone so much as saw their ankles.

We always locked the door. A door that was merely closed was a sign that said, "Come on in and catch me doing something intensely private." Not that it helped that much. Right after you managed to sprint into the bathroom and slammed home the bolt, the furious pounding started. "Who's in there? What are you *doing* in there? I need the bathroom *right now!*"

What you were doing in there, a lot of the time, was finding out that the toothpaste tube was empty and the only roll of toilet paper lay like a half-submerged island in a puddle by the tub. Like many relief agencies, Mother believed that her job ended with getting supplies to the troubled area. It was up to us to get the toilet paper from the kitchen to the bathroom. We couldn't, though, because when we were in the kitchen we didn't need toilet paper and when we were in the bathroom we were in no condition to stroll to the kitchen.

You could, in theory, ask the person waiting outside to get you some toilet paper. This seldom worked, though. The sibling outside the door would always remember that no one ever got *them* anything when they needed it. They would be reminded of injustices and slights going back to when they were six and no one would help them drag their wagon up the steps.

Even when you were done scraping off the top of the soaked toilet roll and standing on the toothpaste tube, you were reluctant to leave the bathroom. In a crowded house, it was the only place you could be truly alone, truly face to face with yourself.

The bathroom was, for us, associated with the intense rumination that comes with growing up. You learned to put on a bra there, said speeches to the mirror, pulled your skin tight against your bone to see what you'd look like if you lost ten pounds, prayed that the gods would smite down Debbie Richmond.

You experimented with Nair and Noxzema, tried to figure out if your period was overdue, tried on clothes. You came to terms with yourself in the bathroom, learned to do what you could with what you had and with the one wet towel the previous occupant left you.

Then you grew up, and it became just another room, the one with the sink and the shower and all that. You could get into it pretty much whenever you liked. It was no longer a refuge, a haven, a fine and private place.

But it remained a place for coming to terms with yourself, for holding a hair up and deciding that the lighting was making it look gray, a place for learning to shrug off the wrinkles and sags, which could also be a trick of the light. It remains the place where you come to fiddle with your hair while listening to the radio and to the comforting sounds of your own children pounding heatedly on the door, asking what on earth you're *doing* in there.

Fresh Out of "Bah, Humbug"

"I wish this were over, don't you?" said a woman at yet another holiday party. "I really can't stand Christmas."

"Oh, yes," I said, trying to sort of stand sideways so she wouldn't see the blinking Christmas tree ornament I was wearing. Every year I try all over again to deplore the tawdriness of this commercial holiday, to sigh and grit my teeth and say I can't wait for it to be over, either.

After all, who can stand to think about Christmas when the country's in a recession and it hasn't rained in five years? Nobody has any money, and those who do should spend it on the needy rather than on another useless cheese dish for Aunt Martha.

This is the grown-up way to think about Christmas, and I wish I could do it. But I can't. My mother wrecked any chance of that for me when I was too young to know better.

We lived in West Marin, and were poor as dirt: seven kids, a dad who had trouble finding work ("You mean trouble looking for it," I can hear Grandma grumbling), a mailbox overflowing with bills. We shopped at the Bargain Box, wore 59-cent sneakers from Payless, drank Carnation's Condensed Milk so diluted I grew up thinking milk was blue.

"Money doesn't grow on trees," Mother would say when I wanted milk money for school. Her accounts for 1960 said that that year she spent $11 on Mickey, $15 on Connie, and $14 on "the twins."

She was careful all year, and then every December, right on schedule, she went nuts. She sent Dad out to the hills for a free tree, and showed us how to cover it in paper chains and popcorn strings, then, impatient with our namby-pamby efforts, glomped on the tinsel herself, tossing fistfuls from four feet away. She filled the house with tacky decorations and Christmas music by Alvin and the Chipmunks, sprayed the windows with snow that never came off, made tablefuls of cookies.

She made it very clear to us, however, that these preparations should not lead us to expect much in the way of presents. There was really no money, Dad had been out of work, times were tough. "Money doesn't grow on trees," she would say again. She caught Sean sleeping with the picture of an erector set in the Sears catalog and shook her head, "Not this year."

A couple of days before the big day, a few stray presents would appear under the tree, and we would mill around, poking them, already making up our minds that it was OK to get just one or two things, it really was.

But when we got up in the morning and stumbled out to the tree, it was half buried in what looked like hundreds of presents, jillions of them, spilling in all directions. We each sat in a pile, hardly finished ripping into one package before the next one came flying into our laps. Poking through the waves of discarded wrapping were teddy bears, toys cars and dolls, knitted sweaters from Grandma, plastic high heels from Aunt Frances. Some presents were extravagant, costing well over $5, like the erector set Sean got after all. A lot of the others probably cost less than a dollar.

Mother had no notion that Christmas was tawdry and commercial. She never thought of holding Christmas over our heads with that You'd-better-be-good-Santa-Claus-is-coming stuff. I figured that something wonderful must have happened to her at Christmas when she was little herself, because to her Christmas was when you got things, and you didn't have to do anything for them. Christmas was unconditional. You could count on it.

Irish? Me? That's Absurd

~e

I just got sent this chapter again, the one called "Irish Families," from a book by Monica McGoldrick. Written for shrinks, it's about how to relate to Irish-Americans when they come in for therapy. "Vague, introspective, open-ended emotive therapy would be very threatening. . . . A sense of humor is a great asset in working with the Irish."

People keep sending it to me. I'm thinking of getting up a form letter: "Thank you, but this chapter has nothing to do with me. I'm not really Irish, you see."

My dad, of course, is Irish for a living. You could accuse him of anything, but you can't accuse him of not being 100 percent Irish, not unless you wanted to chill his blood.

When I grew up, I saw that the Irish thing served Dad well, explaining the talking and the dreaming and the drinking. It served me well, too. It said why I had six brothers and sisters, why I was so caught up with words that I would rather read the label on an oil painting than look at the painting, why the cold described in my books felt colder than the cold pinching my ears as I walked to school.

It explained why words meant so much, and it gave me something to be. I couldn't be Catholic, having been raised without religion. I couldn't be Jewish, like my friend Anne Roth, whom I envied because she had her own apartment and a subscription to the *New Yorker.* What could I be? Californian?

So Irish it was. That's how I thought of myself and encouraged other people to think of me. It gave me, a child born on the left coast of a mongrel nation, in this most rootless of centuries, something to be.

But I never really believed it. We're four generations from County Cork, and two from the Catholic Church. I thought I was making this stuff up as I went along.

Then I read this chapter, in shock. There we all were, skewered to the page, the dreamers and the drinkers, the word-struck race with no words for how we feel about each other, a textbook example of what the book calls "the paradox of the general articulateness of the Irish and their inability to express inner feelings."

There was my father: "The alcoholic himself may appear explosive, outgoing, and charming." And my own cooking: "the Irish have shown a surprising lack of interest in what they eat, frequently not bothering to prepare their food well even when they have ample resources." There was the sister who cut herself off from the family ("a form of social excommunication"), and my mother who raised us, "traditionally dominating family life."

I might still have resisted, pointing out that I had mixed together a few facts, a lot of blarney and an old daydream or two and made from them an Irish background for myself. Then I read, "The Irish have always used creative imagination to elaborate where the gifts of this world were lacking," and realized it was *Irish* of me to have dreamed up being Irish.

I suppose the final test for me would be to see how I fared on the couch. I did go, a few years back, when this guy I liked was confident there was nothing wrong with the two of us that therapy for me wouldn't solve.

I would have stuck with it, too, if the shrink hadn't started asking a lot of personal questions.

Dad is as open-minded as I am about these matters. "I myself have made at least twenty trips to mental institutions," he said. "I don't know why I did it. I must have been crazy."

A Mother Who Was Always There

I've been listening to the "Pajama Game" on the boom box I keep on my desk. "Steam Heat," "Once-a-Year Day" and "Hernando's Hideaway." My mother must have just about worn out that record, playing it when I was little—that and her Doris Day records.

She played "Whatever Will Be, Will Be" so often that to this day I think of it as our theme song, if a family can have a song.

I don't know why they can't. People used to have songs. When you heard your song, you remembered exactly how you felt when you heard it for the first time, and you never forgot the song, because forgetting the song would be like forgetting the feeling, and you never wanted to do that.

"Steam Heat" is like that. I don't like or not like it, particularly. But it brings back a time when we had a big ramshackle house in Lagunitas, and a dirt yard with a creek going through it, with poppies growing up the hillside that led to the road above.

Mother couldn't seem to stay in the house, so she was always out in that yard, hanging the wash on a line or giving somebody a haircut or reading a book. That song brings back a time when I felt so close to her that I hated to use the word "she" for her. Not "Where is she?" but "Where's Mom?" "She" made her too separate; it implied, scarily, that she had a life separate from me.

She was tall and freckled and amused and smelled of suntan lotion, and I trailed her like a lover. She smoked L&Ms, leaving pink lipstick stains on the cigarets, on coffee cups, everywhere, until the kitchen was filled with her kisses. She was mysterious, with her own square toilet paper, and a walletful of money that couldn't be used for toys.

She drove our dusty Rambler station wagon to the library or the swimming hole or the dentist, and always asked for two dollars' worth of regular at the gas station. I never could figure out why she didn't fill the tank.

I had six potential rivals for her smile, but I was determined she would see only me. I wooed her with wet forget-me-nots gathered in the lot above the road, raked the dirt yard into straight lines, brought her blackberries, their prickly stems still attached where I tore the berries from the bush in my haste.

In school, I experimented with stopping my heart: I would pretend my mother had died. For that split second all color would be sucked from the world, and the green leaves outside the classroom window turned gray.

Then, slowly, deliciously, I would let myself remember she wasn't dead, that she would be shaking out the mop over the porch when I got home.

They say it's biologically impossible for your children to love you as much as you love them, because if they did they would never leave you.

So it was necessary in the scheme of things for me to turn thirteen, and wonder why my mother found it impossible to carry her coffee cup to the sink like everybody else, and to laugh at her choice of bathing suits.

Though we had always called her Mom, we kids—those six rivals had become teenagers—started to call her "Mother" as a joke. And we'd say "she." As in, "Is she home yet?" It felt good to call her "she." It implied separateness. She, she, she.

Now I play "Steam Heat," listening to cheerful lyrics from a '50s musical, lyrics from my own knock-kneed past, and all I can remember is the sunshine streaming into the yard, and music playing somewhere inside the house, over and over, and a mother who was always there.

When Summer Meant Nobody Got Older

We are well into summer now, here in the city. Newspapers skid down the sidewalks, Morgan and her friends come down for breakfast wrapped in blankets, the sun shines somewhere north of Mill Valley. An early morning alarm gets Morgan off to summer school, Patrick's in Minnesota helping at his uncle's fishing lodge, and Bill and I have to go to our jobs, cram vacation in somewhere, continue our vigorous program of occasional exercise.

Summer wasn't always like this. When I was growing up in Lagunitas, a perfect stillness waited for us Daly kids when we stepped out of school in June.

We had no summer school, no summer camps, no relatives to go visit. The calendar was a blank. Every day the hills of Lagunitas in West Marin pressed in and the light pressed down, and we had absolutely nothing to do. It was as if the planet itself had come lazily to a stop, so that we could all hear the buzzing of the dragonflies above the creek, and the beating of our own hearts.

I was so bored I once blindfolded myself and went around bumping into my toys, trying to see them with new eyes. I thought about running away just for the excitement of it. Whenever I heard sirens, I hoped they'd get louder. I hoped our house was burning down.

Time hung heavy on our hands in a way it never would again. June was far away, September a distant blur. Without school to tell us who we were, fifth-graders or sixth-graders, good students or goof-offs, we were free just to be ourselves, to moon around the neighborhood with a head full of fantastical schemes, or build forts or briskly staff lemonade stands. There was time for everything. Minutes were as big as plums, hours the size of watermelons. You could spend a quarter of an hour noticing the dust motes in the shaft of sunlight from the doorway and wondering if anybody else could see them.

I don't miss those long slow days, not really.

What I miss is summer time, that illusion that the sun is standing still and the future is keeping its distance.

Maybe that's why the two most beautiful words in the language are said to be "summer" and "afternoon"—because that's when nobody gets any older. On summer afternoons, kids don't have to worry about becoming adults, and adults don't have to worry about running out of adulthood. You can lie on your back watching clouds scud across the sky, and maybe later walk down to the store for a Popsicle. You can lose your watch and not miss it for two days.

These busy city kids I'm raising don't know what summertime is. They're on citytime. "My life is going too fast," Patrick once grumbled on Sunday night as he got into bed. "This whole day went by just like that, and I didn't have enough fun."

He's a city child, a winter child, a child whose fun is packed into the short blurry weekends. Even in summer his hours grow shorter and begin to run together, faster and faster. It won't be long before an hour, once an eternity, is for him, too, a walk to the grocery store, a few paragraphs, three phone calls, half a movie.

Maybe that's why we still need long school vacations—to anchor kids to the earth, keep them from rocketing too fast out of childhood. If they have enough time on their hands, they might be one of the lucky ones who carry their summertime with them into adulthood, like a woman I once knew who wanted to go to medical school, though she was fifty-six. "My God, when you finish you'll be sixty!" a friend gasped.

"I'll be sixty anyway," she said.

She's on summer time.

The Eyes Have It—Twice, with Twins

~e

When I saw my twin sister at Christmas, after not seeing her since Thanksgiving, I was acutely conscious of the Sister Look. Those of you with sisters have felt it: that appraising look checking out your hair and your weight and your skin tone, doing everything short of asking you to spin around so they can check out the butt.

The Sister Look becomes that much more penetrating when it's your twin sister who's doing the appraisal. With twin, the stare says not so much "How are you doing?" but "How are *we* doing?"

This look, though, was new. This one came through glasses. *Glasses,* on a slip of a girl who turned forty-two yesterday. When we all whooped at the sight of them, she quickly declared that the doctor says she has the keen eyesight of a pilot—it's just the muscle that's tiring.

It was my turn to stare. *I* was always the one in charge of having bad eyes.

It seems to other people that twins would be constantly competing.

But we were from the start too different for that. I had a series of minor ailments, from foot problems to earaches to inflamed tonsils to being born cross-eyed and needing horn-rimmed glasses and later an operation to correct it. It was told I would have to wear glasses the rest of my life, but I kept breaking them and gave them up altogether before kindergarten, and my vision turned out to be fine.

Adrian had no glasses, no bunions, no toothaches, no knock-knees. I didn't resent this. When the teacher carried her on her shoulders after some playground triumph, calling her "Champ," I was proud. "That's my sister," I told a boy standing next to me. "I know it," he said, irritated.

I didn't resent it because, together, we had it covered. Adrian's scores on the school yard and mine in the classroom got added to both of us, to the unit everybody in the family simply called the Twins.

Like married couples who gradually assign each other roles, one getting put in charge of calling repairmen and the other of remembering to get the car serviced, we had assigned each other responsibilities.

Adrian was in charge of being cute and leading the class in the standing broad jump and, as we got older, of automatically taking the wheel when we were in the car. I was in charge of sucking up and getting good grades and being inept at everything from getting Saran wrap untangled to washing the dishes.

As adults, we went our own ways, she to the country and I to the city. Like a divorced couple, one of whom doesn't know where the checks are and the other who can't cook, each of us had to find in herself what the other had been supplying.

I got a little better-looking, and a lot less prone to ailments. Adrian, no longer tied to a grade-grubbing, cross-eyed, sickly twin, got sick more often, but she also went to college and got all A's. (She also hogged all the leers from the Italian men on buses when we were in Rome last June, which is hardly fair. If she's going to take over being in charge of smart, she really ought to give up cute.)

At Christmas, I naturally appreciated her decision also to take over having bad eyes. Then something odd happened. No sooner had she told me about her glasses than I found myself squinting at the morning newspaper, complaining about the light in the kitchen, sitting closer to the front in movie theaters.

It was as if as we got older everything that happened, like failing eyesight, was going to start happening to us both again. There's some odd comfort in that, as if my only lifelong bond were getting stronger.

Then the doctor said *my* eyesight was fine. Adrian and I never compete, of course, but I am sending old four-eyes a nice large-print book for our birthday, at which she was, as always, in charge of being ten minutes older.

"A Man Ain't Got a Damn Chance"

The rules are simple. At family parties, my sisters and I want the men to take themselves off and let us talk without them underfoot. At the same time, we expect them to stay because it's a family party, and where do they get off disappearing like that?

This is all abundantly clear, which is why I couldn't understand why Bill, on the way home from a get-together the other day, happened to remember what they said in his Navy days; "A man ain't got a damn chance."

A bunch of my sisters and I had been at my sister Robin's at Muir Beach. Even though we were willing to let them join our conversation, which was about whether or not we should gang-dye my sister Adrian's hair, the men kept slipping off to the beach.

Adrian's husband, Bob, started it by dragging Bill out, saying, "Now you girls can talk about us." But Adrian didn't even turn her head. "Get real," she said. "We have more important things to talk about."

And then of course we did talk about them, right after Rick left, too. When he strolled into the kitchen looking for provisions for the beach, Robin, who had just been wishing he'd go to the beach so she could talk to us, exploded.

"Provisions?" she said. "*Provisions?* Just how long do you think you're going to stay out there?"

Robin, at twenty-eight the baby of the family, dragged a reluctant Rick to the altar a year ago, and they remain a tenderly sentimental couple. I heard Rick ask her, as they were talking about a real estate deal that had fallen through: "Am I a failure, Robin?" And my sister murmured sweetly back, "Only to me, dear."

When Rick was gone, Robin told us the two of them had agreed not to exchange anniversary presents this year because money was tight. And to her shock, she didn't get a single present from him. "He couldn't swing by the 7-Eleven and pick me up a *candy bar?*" she asked.

Well, we all had to have another drink—we were that flabbergasted by the man's insensitivity. Adrian, already fuming at Bob because he had gone off to the beach in the middle of the party like that, told us he had that morning offered to help her clean the house. She had been forced to leap right down his throat. "Like it's *my* house, right?"

Mother, half-listening from the counter, where she was making coffee, said, "In my day it was easier. You just did everything yourself." She used to tell us Dad never touched a diaper, but it wasn't true—we have a picture of him parading around the yard in one, as a joke.

"Well, it's different now, Mom," Robin said. "Now you have to be pissed at them all the time."

Housekeeping was evidently on everybody's mind, because out of the blue Adrian said, "I'd like to have a wife, too."

"I'll be your wife, if you'll support me," Robin said, but Adrian didn't want Robin for a wife. I agreed with Adrian: I could get into coming home to a clean house, with the kids fed, dinner bubbling on the stove and a chilled chardonnay waiting. Of course, so could Bill, probably.

Then, calming down a little, my sisters and I remembered that at least these are the men we have determined, after long winnowing, that we like to have hanging around, even when it's just sisters gabbing.

We all remembered others, the ones to whom we wanted to say, "Hey, don't feel that you have to stay around here and be bored all day. Why don't you go on down to the beach, and, say, why don't you take some *provisions?*"

It Adds Up to a Remarkable Life

A woman called me yesterday to ask me why I write about my dad more than my mom. "How come you never talk about your mom?" she demanded to know. I tried to explain to her that it's just that my mother has never done anything all that remarkable.

I wouldn't know what to write about, wouldn't know where to begin, really, unless it was back in Stinson Beach in 1951, when Mom and Dad lived in a $50-a-month cottage. They already had three kids, Sean, Connie and Mickey, and she was pregnant again. I have carbons of letters she wrote to friends, like the one that begins, "Gaining weight like mad, sleep all the time. Not flat-chested anymore. He should be born around the fourteenth of January."

The next letter begins, "Twins are all paid for, now have to get a safe sec-ondhand car." She tells about having been written up in the *Stinson Beach News* for having five children under the age of five, then goes on to cheerfully describe how she was washing dishes in the bathtub because the sink was broken and Dad hadn't got around to fixing it: "The youngsters think it's enormously funny."

Dad had been out of work for weeks—the carpenters were striking for fifteen cents more an hour—but Mother wrote about how beautiful the weather was.

"Don't have a buggy, so have the twins in a banana box with another box for sunshades, then put the box in the kids' wagon and off we go to the beach. Works fine."

The next letter reports they've been asked to move: "Too many kids." It didn't help that a diaper had gone down the toilet, and the landlord had had to expose pipe after pipe in the back yard before he found it.

When Shannon was born two years later, Mother had tuberculosis. The baby was taken away, the kids parceled out to foster homes, and Dad took Sean, six, who was TB-positive but not infectious.

Mother still recalls with fondness her lovely rest in the sanatorium, reading books all day long, eating meals someone else had cooked. Years later, when people asked her why she had all those kids, she would say, "I was making friends."

When everybody was well again, we moved to Lagunitas, buying an old shingle house on a half acre with a creek running through it.

Sometimes I would sit in my desk at Lagunitas School, staring out the window at the poppies on the hillside, and pretend that someone had come in and told me that my mother was dead. I did it because it felt so good to open my eyes and tell myself that she was fine, that when I got off the bus and walked into the yard, she would be there, hanging out the wash, reading her book on the porch swing, listening to Doris Day singing, "Whatever Will Be, Will Be" on our phonograph. It seemed to be our theme song.

Years later, when Dad quit his shilly-shallying with the question and finally took off, Mother did what anybody would do—pawned his tools and stuck us all in a matinee for safe-keeping while she went out to find us all a new place to live. During all this she was pregnant with Robin, the seventh friend. She found a job at the Elks Club, and was eventually made manager, though it was a men's club.

We never went hungry, never spent a night in juvenile hall. Mother finished raising us pretty much as she had begun—without Dad's help. If she ever felt that raising seven kids was not always, every minute, what she wanted to be doing with her life, she didn't let on.

She had simply done what women do.

Fevered Imagination, Or Is It Memory?

This is how I remember it.

I was about eight years old. I bought twenty sticks of black licorice, a penny apiece, from Mr. Lacey. Mr. Lacey always sat in a low chair behind the counter and watched us kids with baggy, suspicious eyes. "Want a bag for every stick of licorice," he'd grumble.

I ate some of the licorice and put the rest of it under my pillow that night, feeling now and then for the reassuring crinkle of the paper bag. I got along with my brothers and sisters, but in a large family it's every kid for himself, food-wise.

When I awoke, I knew my licorice was gone. I raced in my bare feet out to the kitchen, hopping up and down on the icy linoleum. Mother was drinking a cup of coffee, and Dad was stoking the potbellied stove that stood in the corner.

Hanging down from the ceiling were my licorice whips.

As I stood there with my mouth open, the other kids came in and began jumping up to grab the candy, each one of which was stapled to the ceiling at one end. "They're mine!" I wailed. "That will teach you to hoard," Mother said, and then she and Dad erupted in giggles.

This is one of my strongest childhood memories. There I am, standing in my thin pajamas on the cracked and freezing linoleum, watching my licorice sway above me, grudgingly admiring the joke, squirming under the laughter. It's part of me, that memory.

Yet no one else in the family remembers it.

"It never happened," my mother says.

"Another one of your childhood hallucinations," Dad says.

As I get further and further from my childhood, I wonder more how much memory and a fevered imagination have mixed to give me a whole new childhood, partly lived, partly imagined.

Did my father teach me to swim by leading me into deep water and forcing me to follow him across the dam? Did Connie really slap out a lighter fire on Shannon's leg? Did Dad once step into the yard, his shoulders slumped around the dead dog in his arms?

Patrick told me he remembers the day his baby-sitter slumped to the floor with a heart attack. We still lived in Petaluma then. I was the one who called the ambulance, he said. He remembers where everybody was sitting.

I don't remember that at all. But I know that any story of what happened is always a version of what happened. Writers mix invention and memory to make a thing that is neither, a strange hybrid. So do therapy patients: Shrinks never call your mom to see whether it's true. Anita Hill has her story and Clarence Thomas has his, and truth is a snowflake, no two alike.

Memory, though, is a rock. Every memory, true or false, carries an emotional charge. If it was only a dream, you still remembered the dream for a reason, it still became part of what happened to you.

I wish I knew the truth about the licorice. Maybe I never will. Maybe it doesn't even matter.

I checked out the other story, though. Patrick's dad says Patrick is right, his baby-sitter did collapse and have to be taken away by ambulance.

But it happened to our friends, not to us. Patrick's friend Dusty O'Brien was the one who saw it happen, not Patrick. Patrick had been back in the city for years. He got that story from Dusty somehow, but I bet he never forgets it anyway, the day his baby-sitter slid to the floor right in front of him.

A Fernless Bar in the Family

Some people might say that the last thing we need in this family is a bar.

They might say that even if one of us did buy one—say, my little sister Robin and her husband, Rick—maybe it shouldn't be the Silver Peso in Larkspur, a lively, honest-to-goodness, leave-your-money-on-the-bar, sixty-year-old Marin County dive, with Harleys parked in back, two pool tables and a scuffed old shuffleboard, fortyish bikers mixing with clean-cut college kids, and over by one wall, a piano that Janis Joplin used to play.

A bar without a fern or a fake Tiffany lamp, whose patrons do not wear sweaters tied lightly around the neck, or alligators on their pockets—a bar, in fact, that the customers, a lively bunch, too, threatened to wreck with the help of a motorcycle club the night before Rick and Robin took possession. A bar where practically everybody in Marin seems to have spent their early bad days, their coke days, their picking-up-anything-that-moves days, and where there's only the one girl bartender, my sister.

Bill and I walked in for the grand opening, sliding past dozens of motorcycles out back, hundreds of people and a loud rock band playing by the pool table, and joined my family stacked along one end of the bar.

"Dare! Hey, Dare!" I was Norm walking into Cheers.

And there she was behind the bar, her blond hair whipping around, dressed in black jeans, exchanging wisecracks, yelling at Rick to tell the reporter from *Easy Rider* that his truck was blocking someone's Harley. They had just bought the place a couple of months ago, and had had about three hours' sleep since, but they sure looked happy.

Robin's the baby of the family, just turned thirty. She's been a deli manager, a saleswoman for the Good Guys, a daytime bartender, a waitress at Denny's, you name it, without knowing where any of it was leading. Thirty might have come hard.

Behind every bar lies many a sodden tale, and behind every bar is a dream. In Robin and Rick's case, it's owning your own place, after years of working for other people, having them call you "babe" and "hon," (Rick didn't mind that so much) and itching all the time to do things your way. It's slapping a cold beer down and knowing the money they hand you is yours, even if you have to pay it right over to the bank on Monday morning.

The bar that looms in my memories is the Lagunitas Lodge, still operated by family friends out in the San Geronimo Valley where I grew up. Dad was a big help to them in the early, struggling days of that bar, when steady customers made all the difference. He was reeling from the mess he'd got into, my God, seven kids, and looking for escape where no escape was, at the bottom of a bottle. But bars were no help to him or to us, and it was hard to see then how one ever could be.

We had made it across the room now, Bill holding his beer at an angle calculated to hide the alligator on his pocket. There was my brother Shannon, though we usually see him only at holidays, and Jack Champie, who's been friends with Shannon since Shannon gave him a whack across the eye at age six and gave everybody a way to tell Jack from his identical brother John.

Mother's there, and my twin sister Adrian and her guy Bob, everybody drinking Zimas and trying to figure out what they are. Bill's talking to Rick, and Robin is saying, oh, what the heck and tossing her apron to Rick and coming around the bar. Her kids are knocking at the back door, and a big old tattooed guy hollers, "Robin, your kids want you."

It was noisy, and lively, and there we all were, or a lot of us, anyway.

Some might say the last thing we need is a bar, and maybe they would be right.

It's probably too much to hope for, but wouldn't it be funny, if the thing that drives a family apart was the very thing that brings it back together?

Eggnog, Gasoline and Childhood Memories

I remember a Christmas when I felt exquisitely sorry for myself. I was living in Paris. I went out walking, sunk in gloom, over to Notre Dame, an outcast among mankind, in a coat too thin for the weather and the remnants of a California tan. I stared at the gargoyles on the cathedral, and tried to read through the raindrops and teardrops soaking my guidebook, while somewhere thousands of miles away my family tore into presents and cheated at "Jeopardy" without me.

When I returned home, my French friends had ready their traditional champagne and oysters, and a surprise, just for their American guest; a glass of warm eggnog.

I smelled the rich eggnog and was instantly whisked out of cold rainy Paris and plunged back to childhood. I was a child in pajamas, drinking the eggnog we always had on Christmas Eve, maddened by the smell of the pine tree wafting above the presents. To this day I can't stroll into a pine forest and smell that pungent smell without feeling the urge to open something, without feeling that something very, very good is about to happen.

More and more, I find my happiest, and maybe my truest, childhood memories are trapped in smells, rather than in words or remembered images.

They say that if you were born from 1900 to 1930, you remember pine, wood smoke, horses, hay, meadows, sawdust and kitchen flour. From 1930 to

1980: Play-Doh, scented markers, plastic and Sweetarts. (After 1980, I don't know, the world seems more full of sounds than smells.)

I remember Kool-Aid, peanut butter, vanilla, crayons, the sour smell of a woolen Pendleton shirt worn by a boy who is kissing me in the rain. I open a bottle of Coppertone, and out of the top floats a beach towel, a radio playing the great dysfunctional songs of the '60s, the sun warm on my already brown back, and my twin on the next lounge chair, laughing.

Though I was born after 1930, I remember sawdust, because Dad would back up a truck and let fly a load of two by fours and bits of fresh lumber left over from his building jobs, for us kids to play with. I remember alfalfa from trips out to Point Reyes Station, when we learned to tell the difference between it and hay by the sweetish odor.

And car fumes. Marcel Proust could be tripped back to his childhood by the taste of madeleines. For me it has always been car exhaust.

There I am on a street corner, forty years old, children of my own. A diesel truck rumbles by, and suddenly I am a child, lining up for the yellow school bus in front of the Lagunitas store.

It's so real I can feel my white socks creeping into the heels of my tennies and the cold stinging my ears, the excitement of the coming day.

Pipe smoke comes wafting unexpectedly across a subway platform as I'm heading for the office, and there's my dad again, teaching Shannon to pick out chords on the guitar he got for Christmas, or slyly pointing out the prize Easter egg, hidden in his boot, to Adrian, or walking up the drive, surrendering the contents of his black lunch pail to the first child to reach him of the crowd flying down across the gravel.

Looking back, I am sometimes tempted to remember the surface disorder of childhood—the quarrels, the petty betrayals, the inevitable disappointments.

Then I smell eggnog on Christmas Eve, and I am six, or nine, or twelve, dressed in pajamas, with the cold skittering along the floor, staring at presents under a tree, a happy child waiting for morning.

New York, New York, It's a Wonderful Town

Everybody said, "Be careful, don't smile at anybody, don't take the subway, take cabs everywhere, stay off the streets after dark."

So, before I left for New York, I practiced not smiling. I packed only clothes I wanted to have stolen, and I took a $40 cab from the airport, which for space reasons they keep in New Jersey, all the way to the Upper West Side.

I was meeting my mother, a thrill-seeker who goes to New York every year, alone or with anyone willing to come along. We actually had an apartment on West 87th Street belonging to a cousin, Mary Anne, who handed us one set of keys, explained that the toilet was "slow" and warned us not to call the superintendent, who after many sublets had no idea who actually occupied the place anymore.

After all the warnings I'd had, it seemed like a good idea just to cower in the apartment until it was time to get back on the plane, but my reckless mother dragged me out to see the sights. I went because it was that or linger in an apartment in which two visiting Californians had screwed up the toilet.

Outside, the semi-circle of muggers I expected was nowhere to be seen. The air was indescribably soft, and colored leaves drifted onto the brownstones. A man went by carrying a large piece of plywood. He smiled at us, and, forgetting where I was, I smiled back. I half expected to see Woody Allen go by with Diane Keaton on his arm saying, "What is pretty, anyhow? So I'm pretty? What is that?" Our cousin parks on this block, keeping a box of used clothes inside so the burglars won't go away mad.

So we had a look at the town. Mother and I got along wonderfully at first, the way you do when you have only one set of keys. We did the Circle Line Tour, saw the Met, the Village, rode bikes in Central Park, rushed to use Mama Bear's rest rooms at FAO Schwarz.

We were as nice as pie to each other. I wanted to take a tour of the smoking ruins of Harlem? Off we went to Gray Line. She thought a sunset drink at the Rainbow Room at Rockefeller Plaza would be pleasant? I was happy to board a bus at rush hour for the crawl through Manhattan.

We arrived on the express elevator, out of breath, just as the sun was sinking. A man in a tuxedo shook his head. "I'm sorry, no sneakers."

Discouraged, we returned to the street, viewless and drinkless. We couldn't go home yet because our host was due back, and we wanted to give her plenty of time alone with that toilet.

We were feeling intensely irritated, for want of any other object, with each other. Anybody who wants to get over someone might consider a trip together to a large American city.

I was certainly over my mother, though I can't offhand think of anybody with whom I'd rather travel. I couldn't think what I had ever seen in her. And something in the way she said, "I told you, I've already *seen 'Les Miz,'* " made me think she was finding me the tiniest bit tiresome.

We hopped on an uptown bus, and I made a note, and giggled, and glanced up to find I was being eyed with apprehension by bona fide New Yorkers. All this way, and I was the most dangerous person I had come across in New York.

I don't count the beaded woman who chased Mother into a bakery for snapping her picture, or the wild-haired man who joined in the chase, shouting "You took a picture of my car!"

Then a soft, tropical rain began to drift down through the colored lights. Umbrella vendors materialized out of nowhere, and New Yorkers went by smiling and recklessly making eye contact with one another. We couldn't help it—we had to smile, too. At each other.

My Mother's Story About Sally Rand

The Navy is closing Treasure Island, where Sally Rand appeared on stage and my mother sold candy bars three for a nickel to the sailors at the Exchange. Pretty soon it'll be just another flat island, another collective memory, like Playland, and everybody will have an old-time story to tell.

My mother's story isn't really about the time her and Sally Rand's paths crossed on Treasure Island. It's about the second time they met, and my mother was nearly diverted from her duty.

Her duty, of course, was to meet my dad on San Francisco's Ocean Beach, a highly random occurrence that had to occur for there to be the highly specific fact of us, her seven children, eleven grandchildren and two great-grandchildren.

My mother in her late teens was a knockout, with long, black curly hair, big brown eyes and a tan hard-earned at Ocean Beach.

The way she tells it, she was sitting in a nightclub on Bush called the Music Box, waiting for a friend who worked for Sally Rand. Rand was a star of the cabaret scene who used fans as her only costume. She also had a backup dance group.

It wasn't the lunch counter at Schwab's, but it was almost as good. Sally Rand spotted Mother, sat down at her table and asked her if she could dance. A week later Mother was speeding toward Las Vegas with three other girls in a hot, stuffy van.

Mother's job was to parade around the stage for three shows a night wearing a Polynesian costume and a huge hat. These were the days of movie idols and fan clubs, and she couldn't help but see herself as a star, Hollywood-bound, even though she was sometimes too preoccupied with subduing her rebellious accessories—tippy high heels, a hat that listed in the wrong direction—to remember to paste on her smile.

Like a star, she lounged around the pool all day, ordering club sandwiches and chocolate malts and grandly telling the waiter to put it on her tab.

Then the dream started to unravel. One day at the pool a Hollywood agent informed her she was too tall for the movies.

Between shows she tried to sneak off to her room with a book, but she was advised that part of the job was to mingle with the big spenders.

She wandered miserably around the casinos, uncertain about what to do. She was supposedly a B girl, though she never found out what that meant. Bar girl? Big Girl Now? Between-the-acts girl? Bad girl?

She did get customers to order her the glasses of champagne that were really ginger ale, but these were only overtures: The full orchestration was to result in an assignation. The night she understood this she fled to the dressing room in tears, only to have Sally Rand herself give her the facts of that life in no uncertain terms.

Mother decided that life in that particular fast lane was too fast for her, and she returned to San Francisco and to that part of Ocean Beach called Muscle Beach, back to allowing the bodybuilders to do handstands off her back.

They were far more interested in their own curves than in hers, she says, but one of them, at least, was more interested in hers. He was an ex-GI perfecting his tiger flip on the benefits of the "52/20 Club," the $20 a week granted to separated servicemen for a year. His own rendezvous with destiny—a troop ship headed for the Philippines (and the Bataan Death March)—had been altered by last-minute orders to make for Hawaii.

Luckily for us kids and grandkids, the GI's green eyes and the copy of Yeats in his back pocket blinded the gorgeous former show girl to other aspects of his character, and she put down her book, and they crossed the road together to get some blueberry pie a la mode at Playland.

DAD

The Desert Rat in West Marin

I completely forgot Father's Day. There it was, a God-given opportunity to trash my dad some more, and I got the dates mixed up. "How's the desert rat of a father of yours?" people ask me, and I have to admit that I don't know how he is. He's off the map again.

Last I heard from him was in April. He was in the Mojave, and asked whether I would find him a carriage spring for his broken Royal typewriter, urging me to hurry because he was leaving soon.

He lives out there in his van most of the year, parked on a patch of sand and mesquite, warming his old bones and waiting patiently for me to come around so that together we can turn the country on its ear. "I see it as a race," he says. "How fast you can smarten up, as opposed to how long I can keep myself from being eclipsed by senility. A little time to share after your arrival—and before my departure."

If I had smartened up, he wouldn't know it. Since April, all my letters have been returned. Every time one comes back I drop it, envelope and all, into a larger envelope and send it off to a likelier address. I now have this huge manila envelope to send him, like a Chinese puzzle, should he show himself even for an instant.

Last month he popped up in the San Geronimo Valley in West Marin. The rumor in the family was that he was parked across from the store in Woodacre, or maybe on the Dickson ranch, or on one of the side streets.

If I wanted to see him I should hurry because he was taking off for the mountains any minute. My brother Shannon went out there twice looking for him and didn't find him. My sister Mickey did find him, and she says they had a nice long chat.

I didn't find him because I didn't look. Dad won't call and tell me where he is, exactly, because that would be like saying he wanted me to visit him.

And I won't go charging out there looking for someone who, for all I know, left for the mountains yesterday.

It's a standoff, like the carriage spring that I didn't send him and he didn't wait for.

Just when I was at my most exasperated, Mary, a reader, offered to trade straight across: my father for her father. She grew up Irish Catholic in Chicago, the daughter of a waitress who drank, and without a father at all.

"I quickly learned that not having a father was a kind of social problem. It seemed that everyone had one, usually a bad one, so I invented a good one. He was kind, loving, rich, usually away on business, occasionally dead.

"I haven't needed to invent a father in years," she continued. "I live in California and have a great husband and two terrific sons who love me. You would think that would be enough. But today I read your story and realized that I would still like to have a dad. How about trading off? I'll give you my fantasy father if I can have your real one. He sounds like a great guy."

You can imagine my excitement, reading this. Any kind of father I want—kind, loving, rich, occasionally dead. The kind who, if he came to town, would forget his pride and call you up. Trade him? In a min . . .

What was that? I ought to be glad I have a father walking the earth somewhere, exasperating as he is? Next thing I know you'll be wanting me to forget my pride and take a day off to go out looking for him.

I don't think you should take his side like this. I really don't.

An Uneasy Member of the Wedding

$\cancel{+\ominus+}$

I haven't told my dad yet about my getting married again. For one thing, he tends to take a sardonic view of these events. "We should have a justice of the peace in the family," he says. "We can use the money, too."

For another, asking him to a carefully planned formal event is like introducing a gun in the first act of a play: You fully expect the gun to go off before the curtain comes down.

When I got married to the kids' dad, Jim, back in 1976, I needed someone to give me away.

Mother was understanding. She said, "Invite your father, and you can count me out."

I pleaded, and after holding out for days she relented, saying she would come as long as it's understood that he is definitely not to join the reception line.

A few days later I drove out to the valley to the ranch where Dad parked his car. I bounced twice around the ranch's rutted circular driveway, past barns, corrals and horses flicking their tails in the heat, before I noticed, deep in a corner, an old green station wagon with a lazy curl of smoke rising from a hole cut through its roof.

"Well, Dare," Dad said, coming out to meet me when he heard the car. He wore the usual worn brown pants and nondescript Bargain Box shirt. "What's shaking?" He had been staring down the barrel of a lonely Sunday afternoon and here I was.

"I'm getting married," I told him, as I accepted a steaming cup of instant coffee and balanced it awkwardly on my knee. "I want you to give me away." Behind us, a potbellied stove occupied the space where the back seat had been. Further back was a jumble of paperbacks, blankets, two guitars and a typewriter.

Dad showed up on time, dressed, for the first time I could remember, in a jacket and tie. Bedlam reigned at the site. The cake, made by a friend, had melted in the hot June sun, the caterer had a flat tire on the Richmond Bridge, and the bride had managed to spill champagne and orange juice all down the front of her dress, so that she had to clutch her corsage for hours longer than was usual.

Dad sat in a corner, chain-smoking as if he were going to the gas chamber. Jim explained to him that the rules forbade smoking, then added, to Dad's astonishment, "As long as you aren't doing anything, I wonder if you'd mind helping to arrange the flowers."

Dad did not help with the flowers, but he did, right after the ceremony, take his place in the reception line on my right and began shaking hands with the guests who came through. My mother stood shaking hands on the other side of my husband, a much better sport about it all than she had to be.

The gun never did go off. Hours into the wedding, Dad came up to me, his glass empty and his tie askew, to say, "Dare, I was planning to make a shambles of your wedding, but I'm having too much fun."

If Daughters, Dads Knew Their Places

<del>+ϵ+</del>

My dad, long silent, off the map, banging around in the hinterland, is found. He's becalmed in a little town north of Mendocino.

Certain traffic indiscretions have caught up with him, and he lives now in a house trailer parked on the land of a friend. He has swapped his truck for a bicycle.

This news is two months' old. Our furious little correspondence seems to have come to an end, too. I was sharp with him in a letter, and Dad retorted that from now on he will chuck my letters into the wastebasket unread.

Well, jeez. This is too bad. People liked hearing about him. Some of them had difficult fathers or difficult daughters themselves. Some have promised that if I would keep trying, they would keep trying.

I want to keep this dream alive as much as anyone, but I wonder whether trying was really what my dad and I were doing. It might be closer to the truth to say we were using each other.

He needed an audience for his writing, and there was no one but me. It wasn't an added benefit that I was his daughter—that part annoyed him, but it couldn't be helped. It was offset by the fact that I told him his writing might be publishable, and that I might be able to help him get it into print.

I was after something, too. I got column fodder from his escapades, and thought I would get more: I kept adding Dad's stories to what I knew of my childhood, and what I knew of him. I needed, or thought I needed, those stories for the novel I was blocked on.

It didn't work, not for either of us. All he got was a reader who trolled his pages for childhood hurts, who served as a constant reminder of all the braces he never paid for, of all the children he walked away from. That, and brisk, unwanted bits of writing advice—stay on one subject, stop insulting your audience, rewrite—that made him bristle, coming from someone he used to watch dribble oatmeal down the sides of her high chair.

He would have liked to have been asked for help, not offered it. I keep remembering a day not so long ago when he gave me a gun he had made, and then took it out of my hands when I was fooling with it. "Be careful," he said. "You'll hurt yourself." That's what he needed from me. Not advice, not money, not to ride my coattails. Just to be allowed, once or twice, to feel like a father.

Neither of us got what we wanted. I got the stories I wanted for my book, from the day he met my mother on Ocean Beach to the day he high-tailed it to Mexico, but that wasn't what I was really after. I was trying to piece together something else from this blizzard of yellow paper—the father I didn't know.

It didn't work. The novel stalled, the father failed to materialize out of the man.

It didn't work, but you couldn't say, not really, that we let each other down.

He never promised to be the father I wanted—in fact, he was at pains to warn me that he never would be. I never promised to get him published—I told him what he should do to make that happen, and he did none of it.

I never promised to go on needing him to keep me safe.

If we couldn't care for each other the way we wanted to, at least we could make a fair approximation of it. If we willfully misunderstood each other, held our hands over our ears, blamed, accused, lectured and judged, at least it was real. At least it happened.

And now? Is it truly over?

That would take a minor miracle: He would have to let me have the last word.

The Downside of Being Poor

$\pm\ominus\vdash$

Linda, one of my readers, says she's annoyed with me for bragging about how poor I was as a child.

She had enough of that, she says, with her husband, who told her his family was so poor they picked coal off the railway to heat the house and stuffed their shoes with cardboard. He used to tune her out when she mentioned the chauffeured Cadillac her sisters and she ducked down in, the train trips with their own Pullman car and porter, the ocean voyages. "We were like everyone else," my reader said, defensively. "We had laughs and led a normal life."

I suppose this means Linda doesn't want to hear about the winter we kids slept on beds in the yard and ate government Spam, taking turns telling the bill collectors the Dalys had all moved to Alaska.

Maybe she should have married someone of her own background. If I tell Bill I worked my way through college as a waitress, he tells me he cleaned the toilets in his dorm. If he says his dad drove a truck, I remark that my dad lived in one.

This is a hard country to grow up rich in. The American Dream is a rags-to-riches story. We like people to start out poor. We think that makes them superior. Clarence Thomas grew up in a shack: therefore, he deserves to be on the Supreme Court.

To be poor is to assume a kind of virtue, as if one is poor because one refuses to be rich. My dad raises an eyebrow at me, his once ragged daughter, owner of a late-model Toyota. He wonders aloud what I had to trade to get it.

He isn't the only one. Many of us suspect, deep down, that the rich, like the beautiful, had to trade something to get what they have. Just as we assume that the poor developed admirable character, instead of cold thoughts of revenge, from wearing cardboard in their shoes.

When he was in the desert, my dad drove a deliberately monstrous set of wheels, a 1949 green panel bakery truck so decrepit it gave him instant license to sneer at everybody else, especially all owners of Winnebagoes, those huge silver canisters that zoomed past him on the road. Some towed small cars attached to their bumpers, and Dad daydreamed about getting one of those rusty old child's pedal cars from a junk shop and attaching it to his own bumper.

He mocks them because he's sure that the owners of the Winnebagoes think themselves superior to him because of what they have.

In other moods, though, Dad mocks himself because he realizes he thinks himself superior to them because of what he *doesn't* have.

He comes right out and admits that he is uneasy about the modest amenities in his little trailer. "I must have a certain aridity of circumstance to feel good about myself," he tells me. He must surround himself with real poverty, to proclaim his virtues, his aloofness from the scramble for gain. But he has the grace to realize it. "I'm so full of myself," he says. "I assume everybody is making it but me."

But then the poor are always putting on airs. We Daly kids with our Bargain Box clothes looked down on the Wilson kids with their indoor carpeting, and on our own cousins because they had a television set and lived in the city. If we couldn't rise, then it was necessary for others to fall, if only in our estimation.

And I'm doing something equally dubious, repeating these stories here, as if to invite you to admire the depth of character that came from second-hand clothes. I am trading on my rags like any common politician.

But that's the way it is. The rich get to have the money, and the poor get to have a bad attitude about it.

Dad's Come Home to Roost

—⊖—

Uh-oh. Dad's back. A friend of his gave me Dad's new address, an apartment in Fairfax. An *apartment*.

We kids, long used to trading rumors about where Dad is parked, will have to get used to new phrases: "Are you going over to Dad's? What's Dad's address?" It's the end of an era.

I shouldn't assume that you know the whole story. Dreams of the open road have always plagued my father, but for most of his life, the closest he came to realizing them was the series of cars and trailers he lived in after he left the family, when he was still working as a carpenter.

Then six years ago, just as he was running out of work, Dad discovered he was eligible for Social Security. A man who until that minute had worked for every dime, he sat turning that first check over and over in his hands.

Then he gave away everything he owned and headed down the blue lines on the California map. On the back of his wheezing old green panel 1949 bakery truck, he hung a bright little black and gold sign: NO SOLICITING. That truck was his way of telling everybody to go to hell.

He parked on desert reaches or forest glades, with only a lazy swirl of smoke marking where he was. He was free, and doing what more than one man or woman has lain awake dreaming of doing. The drinking that had blasted his middle years ended by a sour stomach, he returned to his earliest addiction, the word. All day he sat either reading or tapping away at a thrift

[169]

store typewriter, shoulders hunched against the desert chill, in front of what he called his picture window. When he needed a human voice, he dialed in the sputtering of far-off radio farm programs.

"Town Day!" he'd write in his journal once a week, and he and his little black and white dog, Fred, would make the trek to the nearest hamlet, where they'd load up on bananas, dog food, milk and secondhand books.

Dad always had dogs, even when I was little. "Living for extended periods of time with nothing wagging its tail at the sound of your voice is dangerous," he says. The rest of his social life was provided by the cops who dropped by the driver's window to discuss the vagrancy laws with him, and, in a roundabout way, by me.

I never knew my father before he went to the desert. His appearance in my life since my teens had been brief and explosive, like a bird that flies into a classroom and beats its wings frantically against the wall before finding an open window.

But this was a comfortable distance for us, Irish daughter and Irish father. I raged at him, judged him, trolled his pages for mention of my own name, stole his best lines for my own newspaper column. He flung back insults from every hamlet in the state.

It was kind of fun.

We'll have to work out something new now, he and I. His odyssey ended by degrees: a warrant or two floating around a couple of years ago (if anybody asks, he's in Montana) made him decide not to renew his driver's license, and he settled in Mendocino, in a trailer on someone's land. He doesn't like accepting favors but had no choice: He had discovered on his travels that the frontier is really gone, that someone owns every square foot of the continent now, and if you don't have your own place you're trespassing.

I haven't seen him or his place yet. I have an idea he's not thrilled with his new circumstances. Maybe it's time to remind Dad of something else he discovered in the desert—that whatever you're looking for, you'd better have at least the beginnings of it with you before you set out.

I never thought he needed that old truck to raise hell.

Houses Have a Way of Becoming Home

$$\text{---}\Theta\text{---}$$

Bill has suggested, in his mild way, that if we're buying a house, we should think about getting rid of one of the cars.

As it is, we can barely get both our cars into the garage. I keep banging mine up on the way out, because once I've angled past Bill's car, and around the wire thing that protects the sump pump, and lined up the car so the garage doors won't rip off the mirrors, then I run right into the utility pole some idiot built into the sidewalk.

We don't really need two cars. The J Church streetcar runs right outside our door, I often work at home, car insurance costs a lot, and we go most places together.

It makes sense, but I keep thinking: What if I want to drive out to the Nevada salt flats this afternoon, with the hot wind blowing and "Graceland" blasting from the tape deck? If Bill had the car, I couldn't go, could I?

Give up a car for a house? A house tethers you to the earth, keeps you home. You always know what view you'll be seeing out the window, today, tomorrow and next year.

Something in me fights this, and it doesn't take much looking to find out where I got it.

When I was a child, my father's idea of a vacation was to move. If we could not get out of a house by moving, because we had bought it, Dad just walked away from it, or, once, tried to burn it down for the insurance. A carpenter, he spent his working life building houses, but he never liked them much. "Maybe I was in the wrong business," he said once, wryly.

When he was gone for good, my mother scraped together the money to buy us a house in San Anselmo, but Dad never lived in a house again, as far as I know. He moved, with a sigh of relief, into a series of cars instead.

He had always liked anything with wheels. Even when I was little, Mother used to hold her breath when she heard him coming up the driveway, hoping we still owned the car he had driven off in that morning.

Once she looked out and saw, not our old Rambler, but an even older Cadillac, a grand car that Dad immediately tore to pieces because it went only 13 miles an hour. When he got the motor back on, he took us for ice cream on the chassis, six wildly excited kids clinging to a ghost car in the twilight. When he put it back together three weeks later, it went a vastly improved 14 miles an hour. "Sometimes I think your mother might have almost lost patience with me," he said.

The first of a series of cars he lived in after he left was a station wagon high atop a hill in Forest Knolls. When he wanted to go to some other spot on the earth, Dad put the steering wheel back in, blew out the fire in the stove that had replaced the back seat, and drove off. Later he bought an old bakery truck and lived in it in the desert for years, then switched to a van. Even the trailer he lives in today up in Mendocino County has wheels on it. Dad was delighted to find there's a word for what he is: a rubber tramp, a tramp on wheels.

I am not fooled by the lure of the wheels. I know what my father knows, which is that wherever you go, there you are. I know that Dad ran into himself on those windy hilltops and on those lonely byways.

Still, I have something of him in me, something that wants to wake up in the morning and see out new windows, down a new street. I don't want those windows to have windshield wipers on them, not yet, but owning a house scares me.

I am ready to do it anyway, but it'll have to come with parking spaces. I'm not ready to give up having a car of my own waiting in the driveway, gassed up, ready to take me, on a moment's notice, anywhere I might take it in my head to go.

The Years Fly Away in an Act of Trust

+θ+

Morgan and I stopped over to see my dad last weekend at his new studio apartment.

He led us into a large room with a desk, a cot, a couple of secondhand couches. I lifted the cover off a Mercury Royal typewriter. "Ever seen one of those?" Dad asked dryly. While he was still in the desert, he had been disappointed when I failed to find a spring he needed to fix his old Royal.

It didn't seem to matter now. Just as Dad's years—he's 71—had forced him to come home, so the mere passage of time had seemed to smooth most things between us.

We talked of this and that. He got out a .38 pistol my sister had insisted on lending him to protect himself on the road, emptied out the bullets and reluctantly handed it to me to take to her, begging me not to stop along the way for target practice.

Dad gave Morgan a piece of cake he had bought when he heard we were coming, and got up to make a cup of coffee.

He always offered coffee, back when he lived in a series of cars and trailers parked on other people's property. Only before now you had to be cautious about how much you drank, because he had no bathroom.

In fact Dad used to tell me that was what people seemed to want to know most of all when he lived in the desert—what he did for a bathroom. He says he'd answer, "I have a pretty slick system—how about you, what have you worked out?"

"How do you like it?" he asked now, with an ironic glance around a really very pretty room, with a view of the Fairfax hills out the window. "Your tax dollars at work."

He pays only a fraction of the rent in his subsidized apartment—and even that fraction, he points out, comes from the $485 he gets from Social Security. "I'm an old draft horse who always shirked in the traces but is being supported anyway. But I keep myself in illusions of independence. They supply the money, I supply the illusions."

Morgan, wearing her huge overalls, sat beside me as Dad and I talked. She remembers meeting her granddad only once before, when we drove out in the rain to a cramped trailer parked on a friend's ranch. She's not a shy child, though, and when Dad went in to make the coffee, she followed him.

He was charmed by her. I have brought him many things before, hoping to impress him—grades, books, jobs, boyfriends in pressed slacks, my fancy batmobile. Morgan I just happened to have along, since she was grounded and stuck with her mom for the weekend, and yet she seemed to make more of a difference than anything else had. Dad was taken with her looks, which he decided came from my mother. He claims the most anybody has ever said of his own looks, "in a madcap burst of enthusiasm," was that he was clean-cut.

It wasn't how she looked, though; it was what he called her trustfulness. In a letter he wrote me the next day, he kept talking about how she had come right into the tiny kitchen with him, and how much that surprised him. It seemed to him like an infant tottering into the wolf's den.

He insisted that she take the rest of the cake with her, and then, when we had to go, walked us out to the car. "Good-by, Grandpa," Morgan said, and he turned to me in surprise. "I don't believe anybody has ever called me that before," he said.

ADAIR LARA has written three books: *A History of Petaluma: A California River Town*; *Welcome to Earth, Mom*; and *Slowing Down in a Speeded Up World*. In addition to her twice-weekly column for the *San Francisco Chronicle*, her articles have appeared in *San Francisco Focus*, *Cosmopolitan*, *Redbook*, and many other magazines. She lives in San Francisco with her husband, Bill, and two children, Morgan and Patrick.

WARD SCHUMAKER has illustrated numerous books and articles, among them *Mustard*, *Let's Do It*, and *All My Best Friends Are Animals Address Book*, all published by Chronicle Books. He lives in San Francisco.

JON CARROLL is a *San Francisco Chronicle* columnist and the author of *Near Life Experiences: The Best of Jon Carroll*, published by Chronicle Books. He lives in Oakland.